Live your
fabulous!

♡ Eli

Testimonials

"Eli Davidson is a refreshing lightning bolt of authenticity, humor, and wisdom. This book is a simple and delightful way to give yourself easy and applicable tools to immediately live your own fabulous life."

> —Marilyn Gill, TV producer (*Oprah, Montel, Roseanne*)

"I jumped into Eli Davidson's book and found myself, like Alice, down the rabbit hole and into a magnificent world of immediately available light-heartedness that too often seems elusive to too many of us. What an honest, fun, and practical book for working the wonderful wink of life!"

> —David Allen, author of *Getting Things Done: The Art of Stress-Free Productivity*

"Eli is a master problem-to-solution expert. Fun is her mantra, and it works!"

> —Sally Kirkland, Oscar nominee, Golden Globe winner, and communication skills expert

"I LOVE THIS BOOK!!! There I was watching an I Love Lucy episode that I hadn't seen. I couldn't tear myself away from Funky to Fabulous. (I missed the whole episode . . . and I just don't do that.) If I missed my date with Lucy, you won't be able to stop reading it either."

> —Mimi Donaldson, speaker, co-author of *Negotiating for Dummies, Bless Your Stress*

"Eli Davidson is a natural leader. Funky to Fabulous is a real winner and a must read."

> —Frank Maguire, management expert and keynote speaker; founding senior executive, FedEx

"Being stuck is no fun. I'm a firm believer in keeping oneself in the best creative shape for optimum self-expression at all times. Eli Davidson has a winning formula to shake the cobwebs out and immediately start living life to its fullest and most fun potential."

> —Allee Willis, Grammy-winning and Emmy- and Tony-nominated songwriter/artist (*The Color Purple, Friends, Earth Wind and Fire*)

"Eli Davidson has created simple, fast, and fun ways to experience more of the joy that is present in every moment."

— Hale Dwoskin, author of *The Sedona Method: Your Key to Lasting Happiness, Success, Peace, and Emotional Well-Being*

"The one addition to my bag of tricks I learned from Eli was the gratitude walk. Her sparkle, enthusiasm, and sureness got me walking and talking thankfully, instead of full of worry. Her same cheery voice moves you through the book to get off your butt and do something to change your mood."

— Siri Dharma Galliano, Pilates and fitness expert (*Matrix*, *Kill Bill*, Madonna's Reinvention Tour)

"In an incredibly hip and belly-laughingly funny way, Eli offers easy yet profoundly useful ways to get more of what you want out of life. Who knew personal growth could be this enjoyable and glamorous!"

— Phyllis Firak-Mitz, author of *You're Every Sign! Using Astrology's Keys to Create Success, Love, and Happiness*

"A warm, witty, and joyfully positive book. Why put up a brave front? Eli Davidson will show you how to be genuinely happy."

— Sheldon Bull, TV producer/writer, *Sabrina the Teenage Witch*, *Coach*, *Newhart*; author, *Elephant Bucks: An Insider's Guide to Writing for TV Sitcoms*

"One fun book and lots of wisdom . . . don't miss it!

— Barnett C. Helzberg, philanthropist, author of *What I Learned Before I Sold to Warren Buffett: An Entrepreneur's Guide to Developing a Highly Successful Company*

"Eli's work is, well, **Funky to Fabulous!** Her very engaging book is a treasure trove of insights, humor, and practical tools. All you need to do is dare to bring your dreams into reality."

— Ron Hulnick, Ph.D., president, University of Santa Monica

"Claim it, plan it, do it. Life delivers to us what we believe. Eli and her brilliant book help you every step of the way."

— Liz Banks, president, 500 Home Run Club

Funky to Fabulous

Funky to Fabulous

SUREFIRE SUCCESS STRATEGIES
for the
Savvy, Sassy, and Swamped

Eli Davidson

OAK
GROVE
PUBLISHING

Oak Grove Publishing
269 South Beverly Drive
Suite 248
Beverly Hills, California 90212
www.funkytofabulous.com

Funky to Fabulous™ and Turnaround Technique™ are trademarks
of Oak Grove Publishing.

Cover and book design and typesetting by Beth Hansen-Winter
Edited by Carolyn Bond

Library of Congress Cataloging-in-Publication Data

Davidson, Eli.
    Funky to fabulous : surefire success strategies for the savvy,
sassy, and swamped / Eli Davidson. — 1st ed. — Beverly Hills : Oak
Grove Publishing, 2007, c2006.
        p. ; cm.
    ISBN-13: 978-0-9766316-0-6
    ISBN-10: 0-9766316-0-1
Includes bibliographical references.
    1. Success. 2. Motivation (Psychology) 3. Self-help techniques.
I. Title.
BF637.S8 D38 2007 2006932875
158.1—dc22 0702

Manufactured in Canada

10   9   8   7   6   5   4   3   2

Contents

Chapter 8

Overcoming Perfectionitis:
Lighten Up   101

Chapter 9

Are You Baking Brownies or Burning "Blackies"?
Take Good Care of Yourself   115

Chapter 10

Pray to God . . . and Talk to Your Girlfriends:
A Woman's Biological Imperative   127

Chapter 11

The Low-Criticism Diet:
Love the One You're With   139

Chapter 12

Defrost TV Dinner Reality:
Why Settle for Shoulds? You Deserve a Life You Savor   155

Chapter 13

Honey, You Need New Glasses:
Gratitude Looks Good on You   171

Chapter 14

Vacuums Suck, but Why Should You?
Why Not Make Somebody's Day?   181

Author's Embarrassing Admission

"Let's see if you can walk across 6th Avenue without criticizing yourself." I have no clue why that thought jumped into my mind one muggy July-in-New-York-City afternoon. Maybe it's because I was so sick of the Criticism Committee playing its soundtrack during my every waking moment. I had an Olympic-size internal nag. So I gave myself a challenge. Out of the blue, I decided to play an inner game to see how long I could last without negative self-talk.

As I walked across the gooey pavement (the streets do get mushy on hot summer days in the Big Apple) I felt my thighs rub together. "You are fat, fat. Faaaaat!" screamed the Criticism Committee in my head. Dang. I hadn't even gotten to the center white line.

I lost my bet—and decided it was time to begin learning how to love myself.

Funky to Fabulous started on the corner of 57th and 6th Avenue in July of 1981. Not the most glamorous of addresses, but that nondescript intersection is where this book was born. Not being able to walk across a street without bad-mouthing myself to myself sent me on a twenty-five-year journey. I did creative visualization, affirmations, forgiveness workshops, Insight Seminars, energy work, treasure maps, and meditation retreats. Yes, I am that woo-woo.

Using the techniques I learned, I started to turn my life around. I left the Euro-trash baron boyfriend who was an expert in bouncing checks. Instead of getting my sense of worth from a blue-blood beau, I started offering it to myself. I followed my dream, or delusion, of being an actress. John Madden (who won an Oscar for *Shakespeare in Love*) wrote a role into a play just for me. I was Michael Fox's girlfriend on *Family Ties*. I touted the joys of bread and cranberry juice in commercials. Then I moved to Los Angeles, where I discovered that in TV land I was the kinda girl they just love to kill on screen. You can die only so many times.

I used those techniques again when I started out with $17 and a glue gun and eventually built a company that sold $1.5 million worth of women's accessory products. Remember those sunflower scrunchies and flowers on jacket clips? That was me. Then . . . oops. I thought I was such a hotshot that I ignored what I had learned.

The Bad Hair Years

Within an eighteen-month period, I lost my marriage, my business, and my health. I had $88,000 in corporate credit card debt. And no good shoes to show for it. Those were the Bad Hair Years. I longed to take a very long nap and wake up in somebody else's life. No such luck.

A flower changed my life. One day I did something different (that's a hint). I slowed down (that's a hint) and did something just for me (that's a big hint). I bought myself a yellow freesia on the way to work. Looking at that tiny, happy flower sitting in a

Styrofoam cup on my desk made me smile right down to my L'eggs knee-highs all day. That night I put on music and danced to candlelight instead of eating ice cream. That's how Turnaround Techniques were born. Taking even the tiniest step to empower yourself is a powerful success strategy. Even if it looks silly to someone else.

Seemingly miniscule changes gave me enough momentum to start making other positive choices. I enrolled in the University of Santa Monica's master's degree program in Spiritual Psychology—even though I had no idea how I would pay for it. A doctor asked me to help him market his medical practice. What the heck. I knew how to sell accessories, why not a medical practice? More physicians asked for my assistance.

Soon I was driving a Mercedes instead of a borrowed, banged-up Honda. Using the tools I was learning at USM, I paid off most of the debt and moved from someone else's pool house to a beautiful home. My income doubled, tripled, and then quadrupled.

Folks wondered how I did it and asked me to help them. I did. They discovered that the success strategies worked. A client doubled her income in less than six months. She told her friends. More coaching clients came. Very savvy people were attracted to Authentic Success Coaching. In under two years, I was working with business owners, Emmy- and Grammy-award-winning producers, and a member of the founding team of FedEx. I was coaching people at the top of their game all over the country, and becoming a committed student of the wonder of each person's process. I get to learn so much from each amazing client.

One day, the minister at a Unity church invited me to speak. After the talk, Linda, a striking woman with a lithe body and long brown hair, came up to thank me. What I said had given her the courage to go for her dream: to teach dance. Instead of just talking about it, she was now going to take action. I asked her to keep me posted about her progress. Later that week, Linda called me from the pay phone at a treatment facility. My talk had also helped her realize that her first step was checking herself into rehab. I cry just about every time I think about that. The success strategies I was using with myself and my clients could help other people make profound changes. If I can help someone—anyone—take back their life, sign me up. I was hooked. Soon I was speaking around the country and on national television and radio.

Rearview Mirror Thinking

If you know how to drive a car, you have the skills to turn around your day. And hey, once you have turned around your day, you are on the way to turning around your life and steering yourself toward more success.

Stress is feeling out of control. Think of barreling down the highway with no hands on the steering wheel. Feeling panicked? You bet. Grab the wheel and you calm down, right? You are the one in the driver's seat. *Funky to Fabulous* gives you quick ways to grab the steering wheel of your life and create more of what you want—pronto.

Watch your hands on the steering wheel next time you are doing your daily drive and notice how you make the teeniest of changes to keep moving straight. Small adjustments are what keep you going in the direction you want to go. Choosing to pick up the phone to call a girlfriend instead of picking up the closest donut may not seem like a big deal. Try it. Do it often. Eat fewer donuts. Your zippers will start zipping more easily. If you don't think success can be easy, fast, and fun, guess again.

Start with deciding where the heck you want to go. You add to the crazy-making quotient if you are vague about what you want. If I offered you a ride and you got in the car and asked me, "Where are you going?" and I said, "Well, I don't really know," you would probably leap right out again. You need to know if I am cruising over to the mall or heading to Canada.

A surefire way to turbocharge your successful outcomes is to keep your focus on where you are going, not where you have been. Think of driving to the grocery store looking in your rearview mirror. Did you get very far? Me neither. The same is true in your life. Rearview mirror thinking messes with your head and your body. And I have the science to back me up on that one, baby. If you spend your day contemplating all the crud that didn't work in the past, you will end up in a ditch.

Grab the Wheel

Each chapter in this book is my take on an area of funk and ways to turn it toward fabulousness. It's designed to help you look under the hood of your noggin and find out what it takes for you to have a better day. Have a better day, have a better life.

The first few chapters lay the foundation for the rest of the book. You can skip around, but God knows it took me four freakin' years to write this book so I hope you savor every syllable. It gives you the info, but you are the one with the experience. Find out what works for you.

The bulk of the books on success are written by and for men. Women process information differently. So I thought I would even things up a bit and write one aimed at the gals (and the brilliant men who are willing to hang in there with all my shoe references). Success is staying on track with what you want. If you are swamped, it's easy to feel like your dreams are getting carjacked by your day-to-day responsibilities. *Funky to Fabulous* offers you techniques to snatch back the steering wheel of your life even on tough days. And have a good laugh doing it.

The games at the end of each chapter are success strategies that will assist you in putting this book into action. Why games? To make new behaviors fun! As you will discover, play is a power tool for learning. The only surefire way to make a lasting change is to stick with it. And the best way to stick with something is to enjoy it. No New Age guilt here. If you mess up (and I do on a daily basis), just keep playing. Make it fun and make it happen. The games follow a simple format. Center yourself, set an intention aligned with the highest good, do something new or different, and for heaven's sake thank yourself for taking a positive step.

The games are designed to encourage and honor you. Use them as a starting point to make up games of your own. After all, it's you who is the expert on what works for you.

Welcome. Now get ready to have the life you want, not the one you think you are stuck with.

1

The Drive Home

Glancing in the rearview mirror as you back out of your office parking space, you notice the tiny lines skidding across your forehead. Geez, when did those creases invade your face? You look at them and wonder where your life went. Did you leave it in the microwave in the break room? Did it get lost under the mounds of paper that parade across your desk? Was it kidnapped by the weekends you brought work home?

You say good night to Frank the parking attendant. The car almost turns itself onto the street. Hmm. Today was just another day of eating lunch at your desk. Another day of scorching emails. Another day of trying to keep up. Another day of falling a little further behind. You feel as gray as the pavement underneath your wheels. And it's only Wednesday.

Driving home, your eyes may be staring straight ahead, but your mind is fixed on its own, internal rearview mirror, thinking about the afternoon. You were a blaze of busy. Did it even make a dent? How will you ever finish that report by Friday? The hours seemed as tasteless as that Cup-O-Noodles you gobbled while staring at the computer screen. How could your boss have made such a bonehead remark about your commitment level? You worked last weekend. How on earth are you going to find the time to get your teeth cleaned?

Have You Gone from Happy to Crappy?

Watching the procession of tail lights ahead of you slowly snaking their way home, you wonder about the life you dreamed of in sixth grade. Everything seemed so certain when you were twelve. Back then, you painted your days in big swoopy letters and colored them in with vibrant colors. Now your day is made of black and white type. And it's getting smaller. What happened? When did you stop being that sassy girl sowing your dreams? When did you get so freakin' obsessed with the thought: "Does this make my butt look big?" When did those critical voices set up camp in your head?

"Holy moley, when did I get so caught up in work that I lost track of me?"

Are you lost? I don't mean on the drive home . . . I mean in your life. Sitting there while your car carries you toward the comfort food waiting patiently in the fridge, you wonder if maybe . . . just maybe . . . it's time for a change.

Sure. But how? You could call one of those TV makeover shows. They do it all the time. But it might be too embarrassing. Plus, a TV camera makes you look 15 pounds fatter. Forget that. What about the lottery? You could pull over to a 7-11 on the way home and buy some tickets. Hey, there isn't any problem that $120 million can't fix. But what about all those millionaires who aren't really happy? Who wants to get caught in that kind of trap? Drat. And it looks like the traffic is worse tonight.

Connoisseur to Commander

On a tough day don't you wish you could just pick up the phone and dial 1-800-Get-Fabulous? Wouldn't it be great if you had your very own Customer Care Center? It would be an entire department devoted solely to you. Every person on the team would jockey to be first to talk to you, to cheer you up and cheer you on.

They would be connoisseurs of all things you. They would know that you despise rice cakes and that you still keep your old troll doll in the back of the bottom drawer. First crush? They'd know. Yoga or Yoda? They'd know. Cappuccino or chai? They'd know. Armed with decades of amazing details about you, they would be savvy on just how to make your life as juicy as possible. The moment you called, the team would fire up the computers, get a printout, and hand you a memo on the best option in the moment.

Hmm. They might have all the info and give great advice, but they're just a Customer Care Center. They're just bean counters. They wouldn't actually get out there and kick off a change. So who . . . ?

Wait a minute. It's your hands that are on the wheel. It's you who is steering the car. And hey, you're the one who actually orders the cappuccinos. What if you started to steer your life? Not down the same old friggin' freeway, but where you really want to go. What if you started to order up your life—the way you want it?

That's it. Now we're talking. You've got all the same data as the Customer Care Center. What if you started putting some of that info into action and bringing more of what you love into your life?

And you don't have to lose 15 pounds to do it.

As you turn your car into your own driveway a gentle smile breaks across your face. Hmm. Maybe this could work.

2

You Are the Mayor of You-Ville

Empower Yourself

So what do you gripe about in the car—or while you're brushing your teeth or unloading the groceries? What has the power to put you in a blue funk of crabbiness?

How about taking a few minutes and doing something different with your funky? If you find yourself on the fence about trying something new, consider this: If you keep doing what you've always done, you're gonna get what you've already got. In fact, doing something different is pretty much always a part of getting out of a funk.

Why wait twenty pages? Let's get this party started.

From Funky to Fabulous

The way to get the most value from a Turnaround Technique is to do it with some gusto. Give it a full-tilt whirl. You can analyze the heck out of it later. Now, you may feel silly, but that's okay. If I were in the room with you, I'd encourage you to go full out anyway. In fact, I'd go full out with you. I'm happy to act like a mega goofball if it will help you let go of a little funk.

So, what is that thing that's bugging you? Go for your El Numero Uno stressor. Has work gobbled up your life? Are you caring for aging parents? Did your boyfriend just announce that a friend of yours is pregnant . . . with his baby? Whatever your stressor is: See it. Hear the words about it. Feel how lousy it makes you feel.

Got it?

Once you have a specific picture in mind, assume the funky position. When you feel funky, you slouch and your shoulders slump. Tension makes your face look like a sour grape. You look like a wilted version of yourself. It works best when you're seated, so sit down, look down at your lap, and slip into funk mode.

> *Go for your El Numero Uno stressor.*

Now think about that funky thing. Vent, baby, vent. Let your frustration out.

Repeat after me: Funky. Funky. Funky. Louder, I can't hear you. I have done this on TV with Oscar nominee Sally Kirkland. She gave a command performance. You can too! I want you to really let it out as you say: Funky. Funky. Funky.

Five more times just for good measure.

Now, stand up.

Raise your hands in the air and look at the ceiling. You'll look like the Y in YMCA. Say: Fabulous. Fabulous. Fabulous. Like you mean it. Come on, you have more juice in there. Fabulous. Fabulous. Fabulous. I want to see you get an Oscar yourself for your rendition of Fabulous. Go ahead. Put the book down and do it. Then come right back. . . .

How was it? Did you feel a shift? Do you feel more fabulous?

Bravo. I am proud of you. If you did that exercise with some gusto, you got to experience from your head to your tootsies that you have the ability to empower yourself. Isn't that cool? You have what

> *Giving it gusto helps you feel fabulous . . . fast!*

it takes to go from funky to fabulous. To change the weather in your personal world. And it's available to you every second. You have always had this ability—you just may not have exercised it.

It Ain't Them, Babe

Think back for a moment to your feeling of funky. My bet is that it was centered on somebody else or on some thing or event.

Any time you try to make people (like, say, your boss, husband, mother-in-law—add your personal favorite here) or stuff outside you (like, say, sex, status, shoes, a substance—add your personal favorite here) responsible for your feelings of happiness and fabulousity, you get stuck. When you blame other folks for your sucky feelings (like, say, fear, loneliness, anger, hurt, hopelessness—add your personal favorite here), you get stuck.

Why? As great as stuff seems in the moment, it can never fill you up. Darn. I wish it could. And if you try to squeeze your own happy juice out of other people, that means you have to control them so they will give you what you want. The big problem is that you can't ever really con-

> *Who stole my Happy Juice?*

trol anybody. So you never get the happy juice you want. Darn, I wish you could. But you can't. So you end up feeling abused and disappointed instead of content.

Even the very best people get pissy, even the best shoes get scuffed, even the best sex gets, well . . . whatever. The only way to really fill up on fabulousness is to do it from the inside.

You Are the Mayor of You

The moment you decide to take dominion over what happens to you internally (regardless of the gunk and funk that can go on during a day) you step into your rightful place as the Mayor of You-ville. The instant you take office, you step up to the podium of your self-esteem and personal power. Hey, when I say personal power, I'm not talking about strutting through your life like a bad reality TV show diva. I'm talking about simply claiming the capacity that is already yours.

Think about what it means to be the Mayor of You-ville. You are able to speak up and set clear, healthy boundaries. (Even at work. Even with your kids. Even with your in-laws.) You are able to keep your cool with that creep from accounting. You are able to ask for what you want because what the heck, you're the Mayor. Take a moment and drink it in. Connect with what being in charge of you feels like inside your skin. Most people feel a sense of expansiveness or serenity. What about you?

Go ahead. Put the book down for a moment. Stand up and feel what it's like to be Mayor. You might find yourself sashaying, or striding, or strolling. It seems that each Mayor has their own natural pace. And their own name. Folks have been the Captain of My Ship, the Goddess of My Temple, the Diva of Me, even the Magic Baker of My Town. What is yours? Sure, it may seem a little silly, but go for it. You are using parts of yourself that you may not have visited since you turned eight. Is there a tickle of happy in there? Let yourself find it.

Let's face it. You are and have always been the Mayor of You-ville anyway. You just may have abdicated—like the rest of us. The moment you take office as The Boss, things can begin to change. The moment you stop pretending that someone else has snatched the remote control of your life, that's the moment your life transforms. How? You start choosing your attitudes and your actions.

Even when you love someone more than life itself, you can't breathe their air or digest their food. We aren't wired that way. No one but you can assimilate the tuna melt sandwich you had for lunch. So too, no one but you can

> *Let's face it. You've always been the Mayor of You-ville. Isn't it time to claim your office?*

choose your attitude. The moment you grok that it's you, only you, who can grant yourself authentic power, that's when you wake up. You stop being an innocent bystander in your own life and start becoming the co-creator of your days.

Scott's Story

My friend Scott is a great example of what can happen when you stand up and take office as Mayor. The year after he graduated from Sarah Lawrence College, Scott bounded into New York City to begin his life. He was a man with a plan. He was in the Big Apple to get into the world of television. A few months into the excellent adventure of adulthood, however, his sight began to get blurry—and it got worse day by day. Scott went to an eye doctor thinking he probably needed glasses. The doctor shook his head. "You are losing your sight. In a few months you will be legally blind."

Scott felt like he had been run over by a semi. His future had just been ripped out of his hands. It wasn't fair. He seethed with anger as he went to be fitted for a cane, grieved as he started to learn how to navigate through life in the city as a blind man.

A counselor reminded him that yes, he was legally blind so he would never be able to read or drive, but he was luckier than most. The world for him wasn't pure darkness. He could still make out shapes.

True, he thought. Everything was not lost. Recognizing even this little bit of positive put the brakes on his downhill slide into self-pity and depression. Not only that. The long hard struggle of learning how to walk and cook and cope with his world as a blind person forced Scott to find his core. Much to his surprise, who he was at the center turned out to be infinitely more powerful and wiser than the Scott who had been able to see. Finding his inner strength gave Scott the courage to ask himself again: what did he want to do with his life?

Scott decided that his life would be what he made it. If he could get across a crowded 5th Avenue without his sight, he could do just about anything. Instead of giving up on his dream of being in TV, he managed to get a job at a tiny television company. It was a newfangled network just for kids with a grand total of twelve people on its staff. Scott loved what he did. He quickly rose through the ranks to become the network's creative director. Even though he was blind, he helped craft the most visual of media.

That little television company was called Nickelodeon. Scott's creative vision helped build it into the behemoth network and model for the industry that it is today. Scott's choices empowered not only himself but those around him. He fell in love and married and is now a terrific father to two great kids. He lives his life as the Mayor of Scott-ville.

You've Got What It Takes

What might you do if you claimed the mayorship of You-ville? Would you take a few more risks? Would you hightail it out of your cubicle and start your own business? Or maybe take the scenic route home?

You may be saying: But there's so much stuff that is completely outside of my control. True. It's a big, complex world. Most of it you don't get to have a say-so about—like traffic, the neighbor's yelping dog, or your boss's mood on Monday mornings. Hey, you don't get to choose which day your car's transmission bites the dust. Or just when your last pair of soft-black panty hose gets a run all the way up the leg. On the other hand, only you can choose your attitudes and your actions

You can put the "fun" in funky.

Imagine. When you are the Big Enchilada within your skin, no one directs you but you. You are in charge of everything that goes on inside of you. Every notion that gets thought in your noggin and every feeling that washes over you is in your personal domain. (Is it finally sinking in?) Remember that great Eleanor Roosevelt quote: "No one can make you feel inferior without your consent." That's right.

This is your realm, the piece of the world you can direct. Hot diggity dog.

You sit up a little taller as you think of yourself as the Queen Bee inside of you. Wait a minute. You don't have to let your colleague's lame email ruin your day. Who says you are too old to take up salsa? You are the Boss of You, the only one who gets to guide your internal choices. It's your hand on the radio dial; you can turn it from crappy to happy. You're the Boss. Chaos may be breaking loose around you—outside the city limits of You-ville. But nothing has power over you unless you allow it.

Thumbs Up from the Science Club

Isn't it great to know that researchers all over the world have the data to back up your being your own Head Honcho? Study after study shows that one of the biggest causes of stress and depression is feeling out of control. People get stressed when they look at a difficult situation and tell

Crazy-making catastrophe or creative call to action? You're the Big Cheese. You decide.

themselves it is outside their influence. That feeling of powerlessness directly impacts your body. Scientists at the University of Kentucky discovered that stress may even make the brain age more quickly. And who needs that? Lots of other research shows that the stress of believing you don't have control leads to a weakened immune system, sleep disorders, as well as higher blood pressure.

When you claim your rightful position as Mayor of your own town, you take back your life. That's a giant stress buster.

Would You Like Me Better If I Were Somebody Else?

I used to think I was the Mayor of Me-ville. In actuality, I was the Mayor of Please-Like-Me-ville. I could have taught a class in approval seeking. One look at my music collection told the whole story. I could walk through my CDs and tell you which boyfriend went with which. Country music was from the days of the Rebel Cowboy Surfer. Classical music was from the Opera Composer era. Funk jazz came from when I was in a crazy mess with the Bad Boy Banker. Instead of being the Mayor of my own town, I was a politician trying to get elected into someone else's government. What a chowderhead move!

Hellooooo, Eli! What about being your own dream girl?

Sometimes the smallest things provoke the biggest changes. One chilly Sunday afternoon, a Fabulous Thunderbirds CD edged next to a Miles Davis CD seemed to scream at me, "You sellout! You people pleaser! How can you say you're exploring your consciousness? You don't even know what music you like!" What music did I like? It dawned on me in that moment that I was the only person who could actually answer that incredibly compelling question. Obviously it was time to get to know myself better.

What about being your own dream girl?

For some bizarre reason, seeing those two dusty old CDs started me on a journey to investigate the neighborhoods of Eli-ville. What music did I like? World music, '30s film scores, classical music, and anything Brazilian. Who knew? My exploration was such a blast that I began trotting down other roads. I began spending quality time being me, and I took responsibility for identifying what made my heart gurgle: jumping in puddles, curling up with my cat, and fresh flowers, for a start. Soon, I claimed the office to which I'd been elected so long ago. I became my own Mayor.

How Do You Want to Live in Your Town?

So, Ms. Mayor, what is life like in your town? Look around and see how your choices have been working. Are you a night owl trying to force yourself into being a chirpy morning bird? Do you seek out people who inspire the best in you or spend time with folks because their kids go to the same school as yours? Are you a vegetarian because your college roommate talked you into it . . . or does your body actually crave tofu? Several years ago, I thought I "should" be a tempeh-munching vegetarian, and the way I was eating made me fat and anemic. Now that I eat steak like a football linebacker, I am thinner and healthier. What really works for you?

You-ville doesn't need to live up to any standard other than your own inherent goodness. Isn't it time to make your life the way you want it? If you find yourself off balance, ask the question: "Is this how I want things to go in my town?" If anything drags you down, bingo, you have the executive authority to get to the bottom of it and reform it. That's not an empty political promise. As Mayor, you can make sweeping changes. You can spend your time finding out what makes you purr—and doing more of it. You can legislate that bubble baths and crossword puzzles are daily requirements.

The Old Administration

Before you begin enacting new laws, it's a good idea to familiarize yourself with the existing town ordinances. Some of You-ville's rules may be fantastic ones that you'll want to keep. Others you may want to update. An amazing number of rules can

> *Out with the old, in with the You.*

pile up on the books without your even knowing it—regulations from the bygone era of Parent-ville, for instance, that unconsciously drive your choices. Like: "Life is hard." Or, "I can't do that. I don't have a degree." Or, "I'm divorced, I'll never get remarried." Or, "I was fired from my job. I'm no longer a valuable person."

Some towns are run on the fear system. No one wants to take any risks. Even if times are good the bylaws state: "Something really awful is lurking around the corner." Others are operating under SB1284, the Non-Selfish Statute, which demands that you put everyone before yourself. Maybe you live in town that makes "Fun" a four-letter word, even though it doesn't have four letters. Maybe there is a law on the books that says you have to look good at all costs. And those costs are really high. That is why it's so important to go inside yourself and find out. As you discover the rules that don't fit, bring them to your consciousness. Say them out loud. Write them down. Tell them to a pal. And let them go!

Carol's Story

Carol has a dazzling light in her deep brown eyes and a calm, steadying presence. For years she worked as an executive assistant, and her quiet efficiency made the life of her employer an impeccable breeze. She did the same for her friends. Yet she had no room in her life for what made Carol glow: snapping photos. Ever since her hands had touched her first Polaroid Swinger, she had been enchanted by photography. Even now, while she answered phones and did email, she quietly longed for a good ol' fashioned Nikon and a darkroom.

When she called me, she felt exhausted. No wonder. She had abdicated her power and was taking care of everybody but Carol. When she really got it that she could take office as the Mayor of Carol-ville, her entire body came alive. What giddy delight! She could make the choices that worked best for her. It was the beginning of a revolution.

Together we played the You-ville Proclamation Game. Her energy surged as she declared herself Mayor. Her voice took on a new resonance as she claimed how she wanted in live in her town. Her body moved with a fresh, breezy enthusiasm.

She couldn't wait to create her Carol-ville Proclamation poster. In big, bold colors, using words that filled her with glee, she claimed her right to a life of grace and ease. She declared her own preciousness. She honored her gifts, talents, and abilities. She made caring for and encouraging Carol-ville her top priority. She hung her Proclamation on the wall across from her bed so she would see it first thing in the morning as she awoke and last thing at night as her eyes closed.

Being the Mayor helped Carol to gather her courage. Within a few months, she quit her job and stitched together a new life—a beautiful, and at first scary, patchwork of odd jobs that gave her time to live her passion. She spent much of her day camera in hand. You could almost see her delight reflected in her photos.

A young real estate agent with a small budget hired her to do a wacky ad campaign in a local magazine. Being Mayor gave Carol the chutzpah to shoot it the way that rang true for her. Her images were so fresh that the ads became a topic of conversation all over town. More jobs flooded in. Carol's new life using her creativity unfurled, once she claimed mayorship of her inner world. Now she is enjoying her days earning her living as a professional photographer.

You Are the Mayor of You-ville Proclamation Game

Writing down a goal increases the likelihood that it will happen. Have you ever thought of proclaiming in writing what you'd like your life to be like? Don't you wish you had an owner's manual for your life? Now you can write your own.

Supplies: A large blank piece of paper or two, your favorite art supplies, and a few minutes of private time.

1. *Center Yourself.* Take in a deep breath. Let it out. Now, breathe in the good. Exhale the lousy. Do this three times as you begin to feel more centered.
2. *Ask for the Greatest Good.* As Mayor, take a moment and claim your office. Good leaders aren't selfish or

short-sighted. They know that You-ville, Me-ville, and All-of-Us-ville are interconnected. Each time you make a choice as Mayor, invite yourself to find that which is for the highest good of all concerned.

3. *Set Your Intention.* Set your intention to empower yourself. What would it feel like to be in charge of your life? Wouldn't your world be a better place? You bet!

4. *Stand Up.* Stand up, both inside and out. Come on, baby. Stand up. Feel the good sensation of walking around in the world as the Mayor of You-ville. Play with it, even if you feel a tad silly. You are anchoring your experience into your physical body.

5. *Write It Down.* Now it's time to put it on paper! Write: "I, [your name], the Mayor [Diva, Empress, Captain—or whatever you choose] of [your name]-ville, claim my good. Everyday I enjoy more health, wealth, happiness, and love." It's your time. It's your town. Make your Proclamation just the way you want it.

6. *Use Your Natural Resources.* What are a few of the positive qualities at the core of You-ville? What are your strengths? Add three of these positive qualities or strengths to your Proclamation. For instance: "In Me-ville we love to laugh, use our creativity, and speak our truth with kindness." Go for it!

7. *Out with the Old.* If there are some laws you are taking off the town books, write those down on a separate piece of paper, not on your Proclamation. Tell them to a friend

and let them go. The Proclamation is a place to declare your focus and how you want to live in You-ville.

8. *Customize.* Have fun with colors, stickers, sparkles, or whatever makes the Proclamation something you relish looking at. Go for it! Do whatever makes your Proclamation poster celebrate You-ville.

9. *Post It.* Post your Proclamation with pride. The very best place to put it is where you see will it just before falling asleep at night. That helps your unconscious to absorb the images.

10. *Thank Yourself.* Thank yourself for claiming the power to create your life as you want it.

3

Meet Your Inner Neighborhoods

Listen to Yourself

I magine a mayor who jet-sets around the globe but ignores the needs of his town. He forgets to see that his own little hamlet has good food to eat and clean water to drink. He turns a deaf ear to the townspeople's requests as he marches off to conferences with other bigwigs. How long do you suppose the local folks would put up with it? Don't you think they'd find a way to revolt?

It's the same in You-ville. Being so busy that you disregard your own needs is a set-up for a bite in the backside pretty much every time. Maybe you get sick on your vacation, or get lost and are late to an important meeting, or blow the diet you've been doing so well on. What might seem like sabotage is simply a plea for your attention from some part of You-ville.

Listening to yourself is pretty darned easy, and it packs a whop-

> *Hey, if you won't listen to yourself, who else will?*

ping payoff. It's how you get the lowdown on what lifts you and what doesn't. It shifts taking good care of yourself from a groovy little theory into specific choices and actions.

What if today you did a tad more of what works for You-ville and a tad less of what doesn't? What if you made a few more choices for fab and a few less for drab? Do you think you'd have a better day? You bet. And presto-chango, better days add up to a better life. Does a better life mean a happier life? Is it a success strategy? Sure. You don't have to take my word for it. Studies show that honoring your inherent knowing makes you feel cheerier. The *International Journal of Aging and Human Development,* for instance, recently reported that people who have a sense of autonomy and make decisions for themselves are three times more satisfied with their lives than those who don't.

Fast Track to Fab-U

The best way to start listening internally is to get acquainted with You-ville's constituency. As you do, really hear what they've got to say. Time and time and time again I have watched clients find solutions to their toughest situations by polling their inner citizenry. Hey, if *you* aren't going to listen to yourself, do you think anyone else will?

You-ville is made up of four basic neighborhoods: your body, mind, emotions, and spiritual essence. I call them the Alliance of Body Parts, the Mental Board, the Union of Emotions, and the Greater Perspective Sanctuary, or GPS, which includes your own personal GPS system. It's your town, however, so once you've

A savvy shortcut to success: poll your inner citizenry.

gotten to know them, you can give them whatever names you like. Each district is a phenomenal resource. Each one interprets the world from its own vantage point.

Is the Alliance of Body Parts voting for more sleep? Is the Union of Emotions putting together a referendum for more gentleness and snuggle time? Is the Mental Board proposing that you read some of the books staring at you from your bookshelf? How does the GPS, your intuitive or spiritual knowing, weigh in on your choices?

What the heck, let's go find out.

A WELCOME FROM THE ALLIANCE OF BODY PARTS

The Alliance of Body Parts, the physical you, is the natural place to begin. What you see in the mirror, though, is only the outside. You might think of your skin as the You-ville city limits. What would it be like to experience your body from the inside out?

Imagine exploring your body as if you were visiting teams of experts, each highly trained and suited for their job. I grew up on a farm where there wasn't much entertainment for a kid, so I developed a wild imagination. I like to think of my Alliance of Body Parts as a wonderful multi-ethnic neighborhood, since I figure the folks doing all the hearing, tasting, and temperature-regulating must look very different from each other.

I like to check in with the guys down at the digestion plant. They're a burly Brazilian crew. They don't mince words and don't have a problem telling me to back off with the pepperoni. My hair has always had a mind of its own, so it's a bunch of Parisians sashaying about saying, "You are not the boss of us!" I am encouraging my lungs to get stronger, so they are yodelers from the Swiss Alps. It's pretty much a world's fair in my Alliance of Body Parts. But then I find I can communicate better with a cast of characters than with yards of intestinal walls.

Do what works for you. The important thing is to connect with your sensations. What does it feel like to see the world from your stomach's perspective? What does your skin have to say about the fluorescent lighting at the office? Are your cells craving some water right now?

Notice how intricate each team's job is. Go ahead and marvel at the huge task they face every day merely keeping all those fluids moving. Yet regardless of how varied they are, everyone in the Alliance has the same mission: to keep all of You-ville healthy and humming.

Bod-ese 101

Your body isn't just an amazing machine, it's also a soulful instrument. Have you been listening to its signals and notes? Science tells us that the body's systems communicate with each other in nanoseconds. By learning to track what your body sensations are saying, you can begin to access the lightning-fast "blink" of your knowing. You know before you know that you know. And you can quote me on that.

In fact, the odds of your gut instincts being accurate are so high that the Department of Defense educates border guards to read body language. A guard has an average of 22 seconds to figure out if a person is hiding something or lying. Behavioral science has shown that the body leaks information like a sieve— for instance, rapid blinking of the eyes and flushing and sweating

of the skin are typical when someone is concealing something—
and the guards learn to watch for
these key body indicators.

> *Get the lightning-fast "blink" of your body's smarts.*

Border guards are also encouraged to notice their own body re-
sponses. In fact, their own body's signals turn out to be the fastest and most accurate sensors for spot checks. A queasy feeling
in the stomach or tightening of the throat or a split-second dis-
comfort tells them to pull a person over. Often, even though
there is no other evidence, they find their "hunch" is accurate.

I call this internal language of the body Bod-ese. If your Bod-
ese needs a little brushing up so you can start tuning in, here's
how to do it:

*Close your eyes. Observe your breathing. Now scan that
glorious bod of yours. Become aware of your body sensations. How do your shoulders, neck, and stomach feel? Now
get in touch with your legs all the way down to your tootsies.
Take an inner snapshot. Get a read of how you feel so you
can use it as a baseline.*

*Next, bring to mind a situation about which you want some
insight. Once you are seeing it clearly, let your body give
you feedback. Flash. It's that fast.*

*Did you feel yourself expand in ease or contract in tension?
Did your body feel better or worse? Relaxation and feeling
yummy are signs of safety and well-being. Cold and tight-
ness generally mean your body is sensing something negative. A surge of vitality is a thumbs-up vote. A rush of tension is your body asking you to stop.*

What was your first sensation? Yep, that one. Go with that first impression. This isn't the moment to second-guess yourself. The key to becoming fluent is to trust your initial hit. Bod-ese communicates faster than your thoughts, so you need to pay close attention. Go with the flow of what your body feels.

The Smarts below Your Noggin

You've been getting Bod-ese signals from the Alliance every day of your life, but you may have been sidestepping them. Consider your upper torso, for instance. Have you noticed that your shoulders automatically get tense around Uncle Wilbur? Does your throat tighten up the moment you start to express your controversial opinion to Wanda? How is your breathing when you are in the middle of a project with Winifred? When you are sitting at your desk to work, do you take wonderful deep breaths or are you merely nipping at the air?

The Belly Button Bonus: If it's moving, you're breathing.

In fact, one fab tip is to watch your breathing. Deep breathing is a sign that you're relaxed. Shallow breathing is a heads-up that you're anxious. Observe your belly button. Is it moving? Yep, your belly button is *supposed* to move. When it does, you are breathing from your diaphragm, which is where you're designed to breathe from. Your gut going in and out is good. To avoid the dreaded belly pooch, many women breathe only in their upper chest. That means you're only bringing in a portion of the oxygen that's actually yours to breathe.

Get inquisitive. What's the report today from your left big toe? Even a moment of listening to the subtle yet rapid output from the Alliance of Body Parts keeps you in touch with what is real. That helps you make better instant decisions. It also delights the folks at the Alliance.

The Alliance of Body Parts Game

Your body is a wellspring of astonishing wisdom. In the rush of everyday life, you may get disconnected from the natural knowing it's giving you. Take a few moments and give your bod a chance to demonstrate its brilliance.

1. *Center Yourself.* Take in a deep breath. Let it out. Now, breathe out tension. Inhale relaxation. Do this three times so you feel more connected to yourself.

2. *Ask for the Greatest Good.* As Mayor, take a moment and claim your office, and ask that your discoveries are for the highest good for all concerned.

3. *Set Your Intention.* Set an intention to get curious and explore how Bod-ese is spoken in You-ville.

4. *Observe.* Close your eyes and observe your body. Imagine that you're exploring your physical frame like a blindfolded tourist visiting a world's fair. What sensations do you notice? Does your left shoulder ache, or does your throat feel tight? Is there an itch that jumps from your scalp to your chin? Take note.

5. *Take a Pic.* Now, take a "snapshot" of how you feel.

This instant scan of your bod is your baseline reading.

6. *A Smile-Bringer.* Now, think of someone, something, or someplace that delights you. See that person, place, or thing clearly in your imagination. Now note your body sensations. Do you feel a warmth in your heart? Are you more relaxed, and is your breathing deeper? Take an inner snapshot.

7. *Oh, Yuck.* Now, think of someone, somewhere, or something that pisses you off. Your email inbox, your kid's soccer coach, or your least favorite politician. Now feel your body sensations, Do you feel a sense of uneasiness or coldness? Take an inner picture.

8. *Compare.* Notice the difference. What was the change? It may be subtle. For some people, picking up Bod-ese may take a bit of practice.

9. *Vote.* You now have a read on your very own Bod-ese responses. Why not play with Bod-ese throughout your day? Give your body a chance to cast a ballot on choices you are making. Take a moment and get a Bod-ese read on the current situation.

10. *First Impression.* Your first impression is usually the most accurate. Even if it seems bonkers.

11. *Practice.* Keep tracking your Bod-ese signals. You won't get to know how smart your bod is unless you give yourself some time to become more fluent. Only you can become the expert in the dialect of Bod-ese spoken in You-ville.

> 12. *Thank Yourself.* Thank yourself for making a positive choice and taking a step toward self-discovery.

What an honor it is to have met this amazing group! Now you are off to the next You-ville precinct.

THAT'S AMORE: THE UNION OF EMOTIONS

The Union of Emotions is a powerful, feisty gang whose mission is to savor life. Their motto is *emovare!* (Say that a few times with an Italian accent and appropriate hand gestures to get your blood pumping.) *Emovare* is the Latin root of the English word "emotion." It means to agitate, stir up, move out . . . create a commotion. The Union lives for a good brouhaha. Laughing, crying, getting angry—they love it all. They are here to mix it up, baby! My heart is thumping just writing about them!

The emotions are energy in motion. It's your feelings that orchestrate the action in your life. If the Union goes on strike, it's tough to get anything to happen

Your passions stir your actions.

in You-ville. On the other hand, if you're enthusiastic about something, it probably gets done. (Do you usually get excited about cleaning the garage? Nope? Me neither. Have you cleaned it recently? Me neither.)

The Union has their finger on your passion button and their digits on your dough. And every corporation in the world knows it. There isn't a piece of advertising that isn't aimed at serenading the Union of Emotions, because it's your emotions, not your mind, that get you to plunk down your dollars. Since the Union plays a big role in how you spend your money and your time, it's important to pay them close attention.

Don't Tread on Us

Your emotions don't want you to brush the subtleties of your life under the rug. That's why it's so wise to listen up. They can catch important information you would otherwise zoom past. They turn up the icy ache of sadness to slow you down so you can process grief and loss. They send up a flash of anger as a wake-up call if a boundary has been ignored. They kindle a warm glow of gladness to radiate a sense of well-being. Make friends with this bunch and your life will be richer.

Speaking of richer, I know a real estate investor in Seattle who has made several million dollars by listening to the nuanced information offered by her emotions. Carefully watching her feelings as she negotiates a deal helps her tune into how to best finesse the closure. How? She observes her own hot and cold responses to track the strong and weak points of the seller.

Fluency in Bod-ese helps when it comes to the emotions. The Union and the Alliance tend to speak the same language: constriction in your throat (sadness, or perhaps something unsaid) when you don't know what to say to a friend who is in the hospital, warmth and expansion when you are around a baby or a frolicking puppy. As you pay attention to the accompanying body sensations your emotions are less likely to overwhelm you.

For all you scientific minds out there, research shows that squelching your emotions is a stressor on your body. The experiments of Wilhelm Reich, the father of bioenergetics, showed that if your feelings are repressed, your muscles contract. That leads to shallow breathing. And yes, breathing's good, baby. Scrunched feelings = less oxygen = your body's awareness is numbed and your thinking is slower. Emotions are essential to enjoying the juiciness of life. Next time you think about putting a muzzle on them . . . forgettaboutit!

No Need for a Pity Party

Does becoming aware of your emotions smell like a recipe for disaster? Are you afraid of becoming a wobbling glob of weeping goo? Perhaps you are wondering: "If I let my emotions emote, I will look like a nut job. What if I just start screaming in the grocery checkout line? What if I start crying at work?"

Don't worry. The emotions need to be acknowledged, not necessarily expressed. You can feel your emotions and, as Mayor, can choose not to act on them. In fact, when you prick up your ears to what they are saying, you actually have a better chance of tempering their fickleness. You may not have to live through their rebellion at being squelched later on. Just admitting to yourself the twinge of anger when the dingleberry ahead of you in line is still talking on her cell phone instead of paying the cashier is sometimes all you need to let that irritation go.

> *Let yourself feel. It's the best way to deal and the fastest way to heal.*

A new trend in corporate training is teaching people to communicate more authentically. Sharing your feelings in a genuine yet respectful way helps a relationship flourish. If your best friend tells you she will be out of town for your birthday party, go ahead and let her know you feel sad and bummed. It can bring you closer. Communicating what's present emotionally can open up more intimacy.

The Union of Emotions Game

For a lot of us, happy, bubbly, and perky were the three emotions it was okay to express when we were growing up. If getting comfortable with the Union of Emotions seems as strange as visiting a foreign land, journaling can be a great way to begin.

What you'll need: Some quiet time, a journal, and pen.

1. *Center Yourself.* Take in a deep breath. Let it out. Now, breathe in freedom. Exhale constriction. Do this three times so you feel more aware.

2. *Ask for the Greatest Good.* As Mayor, take a moment and claim your office, and ask that your choices be for the highest good for all concerned.

3. *Set Your Intention.* Set your intention to create a safe place where your emotions can be expressed.

4. *Journal.* Set aside a small chunk of time at the end of the day to explore the emotions of the day. Be curious. And be frank.

5. *Ask.* Ask yourself, "How did I feel today?" Give the Union of Emotions time to show you the day from their perspective. "What made me feel bad?" "What made me feel good?" Let yourself answer honestly.

6. *Accept.* It's okay to let your feelings out. Give jealousy, rage, and sadness some air time if they need it. Give your glee space to express as well. If you like, let the lyrics of the Beatles song "Let It Be," or other words of acceptance and wisdom, play through your mind.

7. *Appreciate.* Acknowledge yourself for being honest and open (who isn't going to be honest in a journal?).

8. *Feeling Blue Is a Clue.* If you have been stuck feeling blue, it may be a signal that something in your life isn't working for you. What is it? Is there something unsaid or undone that is bothering you? (You know that you know.) What would be a small next action to take toward resolving it?

9. *Happy How To.* I believe we are more emotionally reactive when we've been ignoring our needs. If the Union is reporting more negative feelings than usual, ask yourself, "How can I nurture myself?" If you want to feel good, do good things for yourself, and for others too.

10. *Do It.* Once you have picked what would nourish you or serve others, schedule it for the next day if possible, or at least for sometime this week.

11. *Thank Yourself.* Thank yourself for making a positive choice to discover more intimacy with yourself.

AN ORDERLY NEIGHBORHOOD: THE MENTAL BOARD

Things look very different as you pull into the Mental Board neighborhood. Tones are hushed. Not a thing is out of place. Every plant and park bench is placed a reasonable distance from the next. Ah, yes, logic is the law of this land. It could hardly be more different from the hoo-hah of unbridled energy you just came from.

Your Mental Board is a genius at manifestation. Their motto is "What you focus on grows." Being very methodical, they can help you, the Mayor, prioritize and interpret information so you can chart out a path to more of what you want.

However, the Mental Board can be very set in its ways. Many a Mental Board likes the status quo. The members love to analyze what could . . . would . . . might . . . possibly go wrong. So they are stuck in the past and the future. They would rather put on the brakes than drive forward into unknown territory. The problem is: Every new day is unknown territory.

Splat!

The Mental Board just loves expectations. They feel so tidy and predictable. That mind of yours scurries ahead of a situation and sets up an image of what should be. Then it struts away confidently knowing what to expect. If your noggin is like mine, it thinks it has created a work of art. Actually, it was rummaging around in the dumpster of the past and hurling whatever it found there into the future.

Splat! The memories of my ex-husband are dripping down my new boyfriend's face. All he did was forget to open the car door for me. It doesn't take much for my mind to dive into the dumpster and find something that's bad-wrong. "The man of my

> *Splat! Don't let your past ruin your now.*

dreams cherishes and adores me . . . so the obvious next step is that he opens my car door. Look at that. He didn't open my car door. Obviously he doesn't love me. But he says he loves me. So he must be a two-timing weasel like my Ex. My Ex hated to open my car door. Ah-ha, the car door is evidence. Car Door Not Open + Penis Person = Disaster. He probably has another woman. That is why he can't remember to open the car door. Yes, that's it, I bet she is . . . in the trunk! He has cut her up into tiny little pieces. I must break up with him. Right now. Help!!! Get me out of this car!"

Your mind can be a sore loser. If reality doesn't turn out to be like the picture the mind so carefully painted, it will try to tell you that reality is wrong. But reality isn't any different just because we want it to be different. Unfortunately for the mind, what is . . . is. The mind just might not happen to like it that way.

Reforming the Nitpickers

Some of the Mental Board members have formed a snooty Criticism Committee whose members believe they are by far the smartest in You-ville and that fault-finding is a cardinal virtue. And they love to hog the microphone. If you look at an area in your life that isn't fab-ified, you'll probably find the Criticism

Committee has set up a loudspeaker there that repeats the same limiting or negative self-talk over and over. "I can't." "I'm afraid of." "I'm not good enough to." A lot of the funk happens in this committee.

Send your Criticism Committee on an extended vacation.

When you have a dream of success, do you hear "Who do you think you are?" in your head? When you look in the mirror, do you see your flaws instead of your beauty? If it's funky, I'll put money on the table that you could be using your Mental Board more effectively.

How?

The Mental Board is a better servant than master. Guess who's boss? You! Harness the Board's brilliance to serve your heart and dreams. Remember: what you focus on grows. As Mayor, you can choose to show You-ville pictures of your fabulousness. See yourself having a wonderful life and enjoying the heck out of having greater health, wealth, and happiness. Imagine this often. Then instruct your mind to focus on the answers instead of the problems. If you are like the rest of us, it may take some practice. It is worth it. I promise.

Mental Board Game: The Solution Solution

Playing the game of finding the solution can turbocharge both your personal life and your professional life. A powerful success strategy is to stay focused on creating positive outcomes. It's one of the fastest ways to go from being a whiner to being a winner.

1. *Center Yourself.* Take in a deep breath. Let it out. Now, breathe in brilliance. Exhale out the burden. Do this three times so you feel more centered.

2. *Ask for the Greatest Good.* As Mayor, take a moment and claim your office, and ask that your solutions be for the highest good for all.

3. *Set Your Intention.* Set your intention to discover successful scenarios.

4. *What Do You Want?* Take a moment to think of something fabulous you'd like to do, be, or have.

5. *See It.* Let's say you want to double your income. Picture yourself enjoying the fun and freedom all that dough will give you.

6. *Listen Up.* What goes on in your brain when you see yourself in those pictures? Do you hear all the reasons it won't happen? "It's impossible." "I can't make more money." "I got fired from my last job." "I'm not smart enough." Okey-dokey. Thank your Criticism Committee for showing up.

7. *Make a Shift.* As Mayor, you are the one in charge of what you tell yourself. You can switch your self-talk.

8. *Quick, a Pic.* Think of a way to make $1. Great. Now, think of an idea for making $100. Super. Now, think of an idea that will make $1,000. Excellent. Now, have a million-dollar idea. $1,000,000. Well done! (Every hair-brained concept counts!) Did you notice how you had different pictures for each?

9. *Brainstorming.* Now, instruct your Mental Board to brainstorm solutions—how to manifest the picture of what you want. The best way to come up with a few really good ideas is to start with lots of ideas. They don't have to be good. They don't have to work. They don't even need to make a lot of sense. Just create a downpour of possibilities.

10. *Write Them Down.* Jot down your Solution Solutions as they come to you (no editing or peeking from the Criticism Committee, please).

11. *Review.* Once you have ten ideas (silly, stupid, and impossible ones count) reevaluate your list. Is there an approach you hadn't thought of? Is there a next step you can explore? Bravo! If not, that's fine too. You can keep playing the game to find the solution, instead of looking at the problem.

12. *What You Focus on Grows.* Stay focused on what you want more of and how you can create it.

13. *Thank Yourself.* Thank yourself for making a choice to discover the power of positive focus.

THE CORE OF YOU-VILLE: YOUR GREATER PERSPECTIVE SANCTUARY

Now you come to your final destination, the Greater Perspective Sanctuary. Inside Me-ville, this sanctuary sits on a serene hilltop in a park in the middle of town. This is the image I usually offer clients initially. Later they may find their own favorite image.

Envision yourself walking up a lush, green hill in the center of You-ville. Let the day's pressures fall away as you move up the path. Notice the quiet calm of nature, feel the gentle breeze rustle your hair, enjoy the zing of vitality in your body as you walk. Yummy, warm, positive messages in Bod-ese are welling up with every step.

As you reach the top you see that you are approaching a sacred place. Welcome to your Greater Perspective Sanctuary (GPS for short). You may have heard whisperings that it's the home of a Sage, the wisest citizen in You-ville. It's a place where you feel whole and at peace. You may find yourself spontaneously feeling gratitude. As you take in the view you notice that here, above the hubbub, deeper insights come easily. "Wouldn't it be great if I could access all this wisdom?" you think.

Just as that thought pops into your mind, you feel a gentle, loving presence. "You can," comes a voice from somewhere inside of you. You turn around to meet your own internal Sage.

The Sage

You might perceive your inner Sage as a wise presence or perhaps simply as a feeling of warmth and comfort. Your Sage personifies every magnificent quality you can imagine: unconditional love, compassion, joy, and even, miracle of miracles, patience.

The idea of an internal Sage may seem pretty woo-woo, like a trip to Tofu Camp, but at least check it out. Give it a chance. You just might get some great insights when you tune in. The Sage represents your access to who you truly are, to your essence. It sees the unity of all and knows what is the highest good for all even when you don't. You can think of it as your internal spiritual advisor, your bridge to the Great Good, always present and ready to serve You-ville anytime you ask.

I often invite clients to ask their Sage for some words of encouragement and guidance. The results are usually so right on the money that the client and the Sage make plans to speak regularly. Your Sage can be a terrific ally. Why not spend some time with your Sage and see what works for you?

Never Get Lost Again

It's no mistake that the Greater Perspective Sanctuary and the cool direction-finding technology known as the Global Positioning System have the same acronym. The GPS is now standard equipment in cars and phones; it has always been standard equipment in human beings. Yep. Every one of us comes souped up with an inner compass. Are you regularly getting the read on yours, or have you forgotten how to use it?

Use your souped-up inner compass, your GPS.

With the GPS gizmo in your car, you simply punch in the address of where you want to go and the gadget tells you how to get there. It *tells* you which way to turn—before you even get to the turn. The GPS in You-ville is that intuitive knowing that guides you, say, to call a long-lost college buddy out of the blue. Then a few days later she invites you to a party—where you meet your future husband.

Sometimes what your GPS says doesn't seem to make sense. That's because it is looking from a higher perspective than the rest of You-ville. It's up to you to interpret it. In your car, the GPS may say to turn left. You, however, may want to stop and get some gas or a

> *Your Choices + Your Actions = Your Life.*

snack before eventually taking that left turn. It's the same inside You-ville. Being the Chief Honcho, you consider the advice of your inner GPS and then choose what works for you in the moment.

The GPS is some very handy equipment to have on board. And accessing it isn't hard. All you have to do is tune in. That small voice connects you to the guidance of the Great Good that is watching out for you.

The GPS Game

Have you ever viewed the world from the top of a mountain? Remember that first moment of awe and wonder as you looked at the world below? Seeing your life from your own higher perspective can be breathtaking. You might even discover answers and means to accomplish goals that you would otherwise never have dreamed up.

What you'll need: A few moments of quiet time. Don't forget to turn off your phone.

1. *Center Yourself.* Take in a deep breath. Let it out. Now, breathe in peace. Exhale anxiety. Do this three times so you feel more centered.

2. *Ask for the Greatest Good.* Take a moment to claim your office as Mayor, and ask that your connection with your essence be for the highest good.

3. *Set Your Intention.* Set your intention to engage your authentic wisdom.

4. *Up the Hill.* Imagine yourself walking up a beautiful, forested hill. Feel the breeze, smell the thick fragrance of the greenery, hear the crunch of the leaves under your feet. At the top of the hill you find yourself in your own sacred space.

5. *Your Sanctuary.* As you enter the Sanctuary you feel the warmth of an inner knowing. This is a place where you are safe, respected, and cherished.

6. *Your Sage.* As you become deeply centered in your magnificence, you see a loving and wise being walk toward you, your Sage.

7. *A Gift.* Your Sage has a gift for you. Receive that gift, whatever it is, even if it doesn't make much sense to you right now. You may find that you discover its meaning and purpose over time.

8. *Ask.* Ask your Sage if he or she has words of inspiration or guidance for you. Write down any uplifting pictures, words, smells, or other sensations that might come.

9. *Listen.* Listen deeply. Be open and receive your own inner support. Are there any positive next steps to take? If you sense that you would benefit from speaking with your Sage more often, make plans to do that.

10. *Thank Yourself.* Thank yourself for making a positive choice to explore the wisdom lying at the core of you.

A YOU-VILLE TOWN MEETING

So, here's the scoop. You-ville is a source of intelligence of all kinds. You can tap into your body sensations, the passionate wisdom of your emotions, your mind's analytic and visioning gifts, and the long-seeing view of what is the highest good for all (including yourself) that resides in the wisest part of you. Drawing on this wealth of data, it is up to you, as Mayor of this town, to decide what's best for You-ville. You are the one with the power of conscious choice. Not only that. No one but you has the clout to take that choice and put it into action.

How do you gather all this information? Since you are the Mayor, why not call a Town Meeting? Bring everyone together to get their vote on a situation.

In some You-villes, the Town Meeting may take place in a paneled conference room around a handsome circular oak table. In others, it may be a gathering in the town square. What does a Town Meeting look like for you? Envision a favorite meeting place where you would enjoy calling the neighborhoods together on a regular basis. Make it just the way you want it. Allow yourself to make upgrades anytime you want.

As in any town, some neighborhoods may be at odds with each other. Perhaps there are no emotional sparks with the Mr.

Perfect on Paper designed by the Mental Board. Perhaps your body craves ice cream when your mind is set on being bikini-ized. However, as you get to know You-ville you may discover that what seem like factions really aren't.

Let's say you've just gotten home. The GPS and the Union of Emotions may agree on making a pie for a neighbor who has just lost her job. But the Alliance is saying a bubble bath is absolutely in order, while the Mental Board is worried about getting to bed on time. Stop. Call a meeting. Listen to each one. As Mayor, you have many choices. You could decide to bake the pie and then take the bath, and get to bed a bit late tonight in the name of charity. Or perhaps do the bubble bath first, then go buy a pie, and get to bed on time. Or put the pie off until tomorrow, do the bath tonight, and get to bed extra early. Which will you choose? Just be sure it works for all of You-ville. Then you'll feel your juices, your "yes," line up behind it.

A You-ville Town Meeting

Does having a Town Meeting sound like just one more thing on the To Do list? Checking in with You-ville can take just a few moments, and it is sure worth every second. In fact, on the busiest days, checking in with yourself is one of your most powerful tools.

1. *Center Yourself.* Take in a deep breath. Let it out. Now, breathe in the calm. Exhale the tension. Do this three times so you feel empowered.

2. *Ask for the Greatest Good.* As Mayor, take a moment and claim your office, and ask that your choices be for the highest good of all concerned.

3. *Set Your Intention.* As Mayor, do you want clarity on an issue? Or consensus and cooperation for changing a behavior? Be clear about the positive outcome you are looking for.

4. *Invite Everyone.* Connect with your Sage. Invite the Alliance of Body Parts, the Union of Emotions, and the Mental Board to join you.

5. *Share Openly.* Let each part of you express its view. Listen attentively. This will help you to see the choice you are making from different angles.

6. *Find Out.* Is there a neighborhood that isn't on board about a decision you are making? Ask for more information. Does that part of you need something specific? Is it seeing something the other parts of town missed? Be open.

7. *You Decide.* As Mayor, determine a choice that honors the greatest good for You-ville. You are the one who makes the conscious choices. Go for it!

8. *Nurture.* Ask your neighborhoods if there is a particular action that would support and nurture You-ville as a whole. Taking care of your constituency is a great way to gain cooperation for moving toward a goal.

9. *Thank Yourself.* Thank yourself for making a choice that honors your greatest good.

4

Are You Playing Football in High Heels and a Dress?

You Have More Support Than You Know

"God's the kind of guy you can trust," was my friend John's advice on a particularly bleak autumn morning. At the time, I probably gave him one of those oh-please-do-you-think-this-is-going-to-help-me-pay-my-bills looks. Sure, he could trust the Universe. He had a beautiful wife and a great family. He lived in a glorious home and took exotic vacations. He drove a BMW—with a car seat. He did not roll his grocery cart down the aisle bypassing the artichokes because they were too expensive.

Are your bills hitting you so hard you're seeing double?

I looked at him with his picture-book-perfect life and my upper lip curled. I scanned my own life and felt like I was facing off against the Green Bay Packers wearing high heels and a dress. And I didn't see any solution in sight. Those dang credit card bills were pummeling me so hard I was seeing double.

How could I even think of trusting in divinity? I had recently discovered that my husband was wildly unfaithful. On top of that, I had lost my business. I was living in someone else's pool house, driving a beat-up borrowed car with a shredded roof because I was far too broke to afford even the smallest car payment, and surviving on peanut butter to pay off Mr. Mastercard.

Sure John could trust the Big Guy upstairs. His life worked. Mine sucked. His GPS was functioning, mine was obviously on the fritz. The Higher Power assigned to him had coached him all the way to the Super Bowl. Mine had left me sitting on the bench.

Oh, It's Easy for You to Say

Being a pretty sensitive guy, John picked up on my inner rant. He saw through the "crash and burn" of my circumstances and focused on all the good in my life. He reminded me, first and foremost, of my health and the wealth of people in my life who genuinely cared about me—like John himself and his wife, Gracie, for instance. I was fortunate to have such close friends during a tough time. Plus my ex-husband's mom was actually loaning me a car. Oh, and yes, I had a small but lovely roof over my head.

Don't you hate it when people cut your complaining in half? I sure did.

I would look back on this time in my life and count it as a blessing, John assured me. A blessing! I looked at him like he was smoking crack.

But he wouldn't give up. I had the chance to be a phoenix, he said—that ancient mythical bird that rose from the ashes of its own funeral pyre, miraculously born anew. He and Gracie knew that in the midst of my challenge was an opportunity for me to become a bigger and better person.

Bigger and better person? Ha!

But from John's viewpoint, my precarious situation was a noble quest. I had unwittingly put myself in the flames. Now the decision was mine: I could roll around in the soot of feeling sorry for myself, or I could start making choices to become a more magnificent being. When he reminded me that Spirit saw my goodness even if all I saw were the charred remains of what I had called my life, he struck a powerful, deep chord.

I thought of Cinderella and the ashes. As a little girl I always wanted to rush through the beginning when she was covered in cinders and wearing rags, and get to the part where she wore pretty clothes and got her Prince Charming. Even as a kid I was a sucker for a good tiara and a great dress. I sighed a deep breath and figured it was time to dust the ashes off and go find my ball gown.

John was right. If I had a shovel to dig myself out of my mess, the Universe had a backhoe (that's

> *Take a deep breath. Dust off the ashes. And go find your ball gown.*

one honking big digging machine). Regardless of what it looked like, maybe a Higher Power *was* supporting me. Trusting Spirit, however, was as foreign to me as football. I grew up playing with Barbies, for goodness sake.

A No-Brainer

What about you? Is there an area of your life where you keep getting sacked? Regardless of what you do, do you end up on the bottom of a heap of linebackers? Boy, I can relate. What if you had access to more support than you knew? If you haven't asked Spirit for assistance, that might be a great place to start. Why not give it a try?

Okay, okay, okay. If you think I'm going to get all preachy, don't worry your pretty little head. I am a fan of your doing what works for you. You are the Mayor and know what's best. It's just that I've seen so many astonishing things occur after asking for spiritual assistance, I would be cheating you if I didn't pass the technique along.

If the word "Spirit" gives you the heebie-jeebies, use whatever word you like—Divinity, Essence, the Universe, Higher Power, Longa Bonga. I honestly don't believe the name matters. Use whatever captures the loving wisdom that sustains all existence—which includes you. Infinite Unconditional Loving Compassion just isn't that picky. Having the intention to access that magnificence is what's important.

"The Great Good" is the term I use with clients. It's neutral. My coaching clients have seen that when they ask for guidance from the Great Good, they tap into an infinite brilliance that offers access to abilities they didn't know they had. That's because they are letting go of the limited view of that good ol' pal, the ego.

> *What if the Great Good is waiting patiently on your doorstep?*

The Great Good seems to have very refined manners, however. It rarely intrudes into your life and apparently wouldn't dream of barging in uninvited. It honors you and follows your lead. The Great Good may be sitting patiently on your doorstep, just waiting to be asked to come in. What if Spirit really did love you unconditionally? What if the Great Good really was eager to help you unfold the dreams written in your heart? What if God truly was the type of guy you could trust?

When I forget to ask for help, I feel like such a numbskull, because I've been blessed to see God's grace painted all over my life. But I come from a long line of headstrong women. (My mom claims that her first words were "I'll do it myself." Since Aunt Nancy always nods in agreement, it's probably true.) Doing it myself is in my nature—which is how I ended up falling into more than one of life's holes.

Denial Is Not Just a River in Egypt

For more than a decade, money was the area that had me stumped. Even though I had a college degree from a good school, there were times when a bunch of brown coins was all I had in my wallet. My strategy for handling the fiscal chaos I created was simple. I stayed unconscious.

Denial is not just a river in Egypt. It was the watchword of my financial life. I would open a checking account, and when the checks started to bounce I would go to another bank and open another account. Why bother balancing a checkbook? I was lousy at math. When checks bounced at the new bank, I knew I was out of money again. (I don't think I fully understood how completely insane this was until I started speaking before groups. There were gasps from the audience every time I told this part of the story.)

The Great Good isn't too busy to be your partner.

Paying off my credit cards seemed as impossible as trying to kick a field goal holding down a mini skirt. (Just like in football, the penalties were killing me.) As soon as I sent in a payment, there was another huge defensive tackle of a statement waiting to sack me. I would make money from acting jobs and blow it quickly. Then, like 98 percent of all actors, I would take lousy, low-paying jobs between acting gigs. A bounced check was like the referee blowing the whistle that I had run out of bounds once more.

I felt completely hopeless. I had proved over and over that I wouldn't get very far financially left to my own devices. Acting jobs got further and further apart, and my ability to pay my bills kept diminishing. I didn't have any marketable skills except for my knowledge of Shakespeare, darn good comedic timing, and a killer Indian accent. Needless to say, the corporate job offers weren't exactly rolling in.

It was about this time that John introduced me to the concept of inviting the Great Good to be my partner. *Hmmm, does that mean having the Divine Being who created and loves all as my colleague?* I had thought the Creator was far too busy running the Universe to take a day-to-day interest in little ol' me. Look at all those tropical fish that are still getting discovered. Look at all the new electronic gizmos that are getting invented. . . . I figured he had his hands full. Besides, my silly little questions weren't profound or spiritual enough. But, what the heck, I decided to give it a whirl.

Onto the Playing Field

So, I invited the Great Good to get down out of that dang Goodyear Blimp and onto the playing field of my everyday life. Instead of hanging up there and taking play-by-play aerial shots, I wanted the Great Good to get down here in the game. "Come on, GG, put on some pads and cleats and go kick some butt" was my attitude. Gee, what a surprise. Spirit let me know that it isn't in the butt-kicking game, it's in the loving and forgiveness game. A gentle inner voice reminded me that I had all the talents and skills to make my own touchdowns, that even if I didn't believe it myself, the Great Good did. In fact, Spirit and I could do it together.

> *Yes, WE can.*

I remember taping up a little sign in my bathroom: "Yes, WE can." It was so comforting to think I had a powerful ally. My tiny sign gave me a bit more confidence every day. My trouble wasn't that I was hopeless. I had just been trying to do it myself. At some point I turned the corner and decided to listen to the Great Good's guidance because, what the heck, he invented football.

To be honest, I have never understood the allure of men in tights and helmets pummeling each other for a piece of pigskin. What's the big deal about a bunch of guys piling onto each other every time the whistle blows? My brother Seth used to sit next to me so he could point out where the ball was. I was equally clueless when it came to having faith in my Higher Power. Being a regular couch potato in the trust department, I realized I needed to pump some "trust iron" to develop my ability to believe that Spirit would actually assist me.

Trust-ercize

Just like someone starting an exercise program at the gym, I took it slow. I started by asking for Spirit's assistance with small things, like finding a parking place. (You may laugh. But in L.A. getting a parking place within a few blocks of a popular coffee house requires a small miracle.) Asking the Universe to help me find a parking place was like lifting 5-pound barbells. It wasn't much, but at least I was starting somewhere. I would ask for a parking angel . . . and voilà! Someone would start pulling out of a parking space.

It was so much fun to watch the mini-miracles. I graduated to circuit training. I started asking the Great Good's guidance at the beginning of the day, and I kept a journal of the blessings that showed up. Just like when you're training at the gym, trust seemed to grow at its own pace. Sometimes I would get clear advice. Other times I seemed to get nothing. Strangely enough, the times of silence ended up teaching me a lot. I learned about patience and letting go of being in control. The blessings showed up in their own time, not mine.

My journal was called: "Is it odd or is it God?" I tracked the issue I wanted help with, how I asked, and the result. Being able to look back at pages filled with phenomenal coincidences of good fortune helped me. When I started doubting if the whole trusting the Great Good thing worked, I could look at the track record. My trust capacity grew. Within a few months of actively working at it, I began to have confidence in listening to my inner guidance.

The Big Money Miracle

One day, for some apparently unknown reason, I got a flash. "Go do something new" was the message. Since I had been having such good results following these small inspirations, I wondered how I could check it out. "Hmmm. Do something new . . . but what?" Then a shopportunity moment hit me. I had seen a gorgeous hair doodad that was out of my budget. Even though I had no clue how to do it, I figured maybe I could make one myself. That would sure be something new.

My trust muscles stretched as I ventured into the strange world of a crafts supply store. I bought a glue gun and glued some red silk roses on a barrette. The roses were so beautifully made that they looked like they had just been picked from a garden. I had never operated a glue gun, and I don't think I had ever bought silk flowers before. But there was such an easy flow, as though I was guided to do it.

I was so proud of my little creation that I wore it everywhere. Later that week, I walked through an elite Los Angeles store, Fred Segal, my new barrette in my hair. It was my sumptuous adornment that gave me the confidence to walk into such a swanky place. Much to my shock, one of the Fred Segal buyers saw it, stopped me, and asked if she could purchase the item in quantity for the store. I sold $1000 worth the first week. That was Big Money to me at the time. Orders from other stores came flooding in. Soon I was creating other designs. I made a barrette with sunflowers (the state flower of my home state, Kansas), and even more orders poured in.

Ask. Listen. Take a small step.

Within six months, my original red rose barrette was featured in *Women's Wear Daily*—the *Wall Street Journal* of the fashion business. I was a nationally recognized accessory designer. Within two years I had showrooms all over the country and was selling my designs in over 1,000 stores nationwide. No experience. No degree. Not a single design class. But I was fortunate to have the best business partner. By inviting the Great Good's guidance, I had opened up to a wealth of ingenuity and talents I hadn't known were within me. During those days I often faced situations that seemed completely impossible. But I sure knew that if I couldn't figure it out, the Great Good could.

For the first time in my adult life I was out of the cycle of lack of funds. When I got out of the way and let the Great Good have a say, my life was transformed. First step: I asked for spiritual assistance. Second step: I listened to my inner guidance. Third step: I took a small action—I went to a crafts store. The success strategy was easy, fast, and fun.

I couldn't tell you why it works. But then again, I couldn't tell you why electricity works, yet that doesn't stop either you or me from firing up the washer-dryer. Take it from me: give it a try and see what happens. What would a beginner class at the Trust Gym be like for you? You might discover that God is the kinda guy, or gal, you can trust.

The Invitation Game

If you have never considered asking Spirit for assistance, this may feel a bit odd. But you really can't mess up when you are talking to the Great Good. There's no wrong way to play or pray, especially when you ask for only that which is for the highest good of all concerned.

1. *Center Yourself.* Take in a deep breath. Let it out. Now, breathe in infinite good. Exhale self-doubt. Do this three times so you feel more open.

2. *Invite the Greatest Good.* Invite yourself to align with whatever is the highest good of all concerned.

3. *Set Your Intention.* As Mayor, take a moment and be open to receive spiritual assistance.

4. *Ask.* Ask for support in some area of your life that's been a challenge.

5. *Start Small.* Now, don't pull a hamstring. If you are new to this, start with something little, like . . . the DVD you want to rent is finally in stock.

6. *Take Five.* Take a few moments to be open to a response. Listen in the quiet for any inner guidance that comes. (You might be guided to a new lunch spot and bump into a chum you've been playing phone tag with for a month.)

7. *Check It Out.* If you get positive advice, check it out. That is, take a small step toward doing it. If it seems to be right, continue. Using your common sense, of

course. Don't do anything that might harm you or anyone else.

8. *Keep Track.* Record in your journal what you asked for and what showed up. That way you can check the stats over time.

9. *Thank Yourself.* Thank yourself for making a positive choice to invite spiritual support.

5

Don't Feed the Lizard

What to Do with Your Nagging Fears

Does dread sometimes grip you for no reason? Are you haunted by fears that something terrible is about to happen? Are you paralyzed with panic when you think about doing something new? No, you're not losing your mind. The Fright Factor that's making you freeze is merely the lizard in your head hogging the stage.

The *lizard?*

Yes, my dear, the lizard. You have a reptile living deep in your head. It's called your reptilian brain, and it's a remnant of your genetic past. It's powerful and has a great sense of drama, but sometimes it's just not all that bright.

Here's the deal: Almost every single one of those fear signals in your head is a false alarm. A False Alarm. (I'm saying it twice so it will sink in.) Fear is funk.

> *Tame the lizard in your head.*

When you make a decision based on the voice of fear, you're running down the road to funk. Yep, that little reptile could be running you ragged. Negative thinking is a very powerful way to sabotage your success. A surefire way to move toward more of what you want is to observe and disassemble the fears that stand in your way.

Learning a wee bit about your head reptile will help you put a muzzle on it. So buckle your seat belt. I'm taking you on a tour of your noggin. I'm going give you all the info you need to dismantle your Fear Factor for good.

The Big Three

Paul MacLean, former director of the Laboratory of Brain Evolution at the National Institute of Mental Health and author of *The Triune Brain in Evolution,* explains that the human brain is really three brains in one. Each brain evolved at a different step of our evolution.

The simplest and most primitive brain is called the R-complex, or reptilian brain, because of its similarity to the brain in reptiles. It controls our basic survival and is essentially fear-based (just think of how reptiles behave). The second brain, the limbic system, is similar to the brain in lower mammals and seems to be the seat of our emotions, personal identity, and some aspects of memory. The third and most recently evolved brain, the neocortex, is devoted to higher-order thinking, verbal memory, more complicated reasoning, as well as those handy linguistic skills that *Homo sapiens* is known for.

MacLean says the three brains operate like "three interconnected biological computers, with each having its own special intelligence, its own subjectivity, its own sense of time and space, and its own memory, motor, and other functions." You might think the neocortex runs the other two brains, but no. In any given moment, any one of the three brains dominates the others. That's one of the reasons we humans are so darn complex.

Your Deep Dark Inner . . . Reptile

The reptilian brain, for all its lowliness, is no wimp. It is so fundamental to our existence that educational innovator and researcher Elaine de Beauport calls it the basic brain. It is the first part of the brain to develop in the womb. And it is buried the deepest in the head so it is the last to sustain injury.

It's the part of your brain that's in charge of self-preservation and the preservation of the species. It governs primary functions like your heart rate, breathing, blood pressure, and body temperature. It's the one that's still running while you are asleep. It is also the part of your brain that sets off your automatic responses. If you want to watch your basic brain in action, step outside on a bright sunny day with a mirror in your hand. Watch how your pupils dilate . . . without your ever thinking about it. The basic brain is programmed to respond before you think.

The reptilian brain also has the task of sorting through the onslaught of data coming in through your five senses and up the spinal cord into the brain at large—at a rate of 100 million impulses per second. Besides signaling all the folks at the Alliance of Body Parts to get busy adjusting your body functions, it figures out what crucial information to send upstairs to the limbic system and the neocortex, and what to put aside. How does it handle so much input? By concocting a filing system of patterns, assumptions, and habits, most of which get set in place during your earliest years. The choices it makes determine how you translate what's happening in the external world into your own internal experience, the subjective context in which you live.

Speed, Not Smarts

Your lizard may be powerful, but it isn't always very smart. I have never met one that could read, for that matter. It files the records of past threats both real and imagined in the same folder (because it can't tell the difference). Since its primary concern is your survival moment to moment, it monitors every sensation for potential hazard. The trouble is, it can't distinguish between what is likely to kill you and what will merely chip your fingernail.

Thanks, evolution! Genetics has made us into worry warts.

Watch a lizard sometime. Living here in Southern California, I have a number of them in my backyard. The lizard sits there, basking in the sun, its senses always on guard duty. At the mere *hint* of a possible menace (like the sudden movement of shadow), it is gone lickety-split. You can't blame it. In the reptile world parents don't nurture their young, they eat them. Baby lizards look like lunch to their moms. No wonder the poor lizard in your head is a bit paranoid.

Thanks, evolution! Now we have a finely tuned genetic mechanism that turns us into . . . worry warts.

Back When Life Was Simple: Eat or Be Eaten

When the scaly little creature in your head sees a potentially dangerous piece of data coming in, it pushes the panic button. Buzzers go off, and your body switches into the phenomenon known as the fight-or-flight response. A ton of research has been done on the effects of this response on the body.

When you sense danger, your adrenal glands dump epinephrine and norepinephrine into the bloodstream. Those powerful stress hormones helped your great-great-great-great-times-one-thousand grandmother run her best time ever to escape becoming a saber-toothed tiger's mid-afternoon snack. The folks with a quick hand on the fight-or-flight button were the ones who stuck around long enough to pass their genes on to the next generation. You inherited those genes. That's why you have an inborn sensor scanning the world for the slightest whiff of harm.

However, these days your panic button, designed to save you from significant threats to life and limb, gets used for trifles. Realizing that you lost your PDA is a pain in the neck. Not a potential cause of death. But your reptilian brain doesn't know that. It pushes the panic button just the same. That's its job. Suddenly the run-for-the-hills stress hormones are coursing through your bloodstream. But since you are just sitting and fuming in your car in the mall parking lot, those chemicals are backing up inside you instead of being burned off.

An excess of those hormones can make you prone to heart disease, a weakened immune system, high blood pressure, and other physical ailments. Studies show that higher levels of epinephrine even encourage weight gain. Yes, baby doll, stress can make you fat! And who needs that?

The Hidden Drama Queen

The talent your lizard lacks in the file room is made up for by her ability to dramatize. She scans your world looking for catastrophe the way an actress looks for a publicity stunt. She reads "Warning! Danger!" into just about anything. She doesn't stop to ask if it is real or imaginary. Who cares? She has great lines and she's going with it.

Think of a juicy, fragrant lemon. Now think of a gray-haired woman slicing it in half. See her offering you the sparkling lemon and inviting you to take a bite. Do you feel your saliva glands beginning to work? If you are like most people, your mouth now has quite a bit more saliva going than a paragraph ago. That's your inner reptile pushing and pulling the levers again.

There's a Calamity Jane in your brain.

Besides responding to the scent of the lemon, your inner gecko is also noting the imminent hazard of an old lady brandishing a knife. As it hands your autonomic nervous system a quick memo: "Beware of cranky old ladies clutching knives," does your mind conjure scenes from a horror flick, and do you feel your heart begin to pound? That is "catastrophizing"—imagining a catastrophe when there isn't one. Your head lizard is a master at that sort of thing. She's the one who loves to scream at Wes Craven movies.

Why let a starlet drive your life? The only time to let your frightened reptile have its way is when you're standing in front of an oncoming bus. And how often is that?

Why Let Your Past Ruin Your Now?

Your basic brain is a genius at generalization. If your ancestors once escaped from a mastodon that was hiding behind a large brown boulder, that brain cued them to be extra careful every time they trotted past a large brown boulder. Being cautious when passing the large brown boulder saved many a cave person. Your lizard is still milking the drama.

Yet generalizations are rarely accurate. In fact, most of them are completely bogus. Let's say a blonde-haired, blue-eyed guy named Mike broke your heart 15 years ago, and I introduce you to a spiritual stud muffin who happens to be another blonde-haired, blue-eyed guy named Mike. Even though this year's model could be the kindest man on the planet, if your basic brain has categorized blonde-haired, blue-eyed Mikes in the P for Pain folder, you might bolt—and miss a wonderful relationship.

Put red-alert buzzers around generalizations. They are fear speaking. "I never get ahead at work," "Politicians are louses," "I can never stay on a diet" are some common ones. What are some of yours? The next time you hear yourself making a sweeping generalization, take a moment. "Push the pause button," as my author-friend Mimi Donaldson says, and see if what you are saying is really real. You may find out that the cagey reptile in your head is reacting before the other parts of you have had a chance to speak up.

Stranger than Fiction: A Miracle in a Shoebox

Jaime walked around in her life as if someone had let most of the air out of her tires. She went to work and came home. She didn't have deep friendships. She was plagued by the memory that she was not wanted as a child. And the fact that her parents never came to a single one of her school musicals was the proof.

One day she collected her courage and confronted her parents. "I don't really think that either of you cared about what was important to me. Music was my life. Why didn't you ever come to any of my performances?" she asked them.

Strange but true: Memory can be fact or fiction.

Both parents looked at her in stunned silence. Her mom shook her head, slowly left the room, and returned with a shoebox. Opening the box, she pulled out photo after photo. Jaime began to sob as she looked at the photographs and the programs. There she was with her parents . . . at her performances.

Jaime's parents had attended almost every one of her shows. Strangely, for some unknown reason her inner reptile had discarded those memories. Impossible as it seems, what you remember may be a long way from fact. That's one reason I encourage my clients to stay with what is currently happening in their lives and what they want to manifest.

You don't have to believe everything you think. Before you blow off an opportunity, do yourself a favor and check it out. Ask questions. Why not give it the benefit of the doubt? Why not take a chance on opening your heart to that very kind blonde-haired, blue-eyed guy named Mike?

Fear Is Lizard Food

When you feed something, it grows. Every time you listen to your fear, you are feeding your lizard. Every time you react out of a place of dread, you are feeding your lizard. Every time you make a generalization without checking out the facts, you are feeding your lizard. Every time you take an action based in fear, you are feeding your lizard a double portion.

As de Beauport says, "You are the conductor of your brain." The next time you feel paralyzed by fear ask yourself, "Am I going to let a small reptile take over You-ville?" Heck no! You are the Mayor. Thank the reptile in your head for the good job it's doing keeping everything running, but you are the one in charge of the town.

As an override to Lizzie the Lizard's fear filter downstairs in the deep brain, try putting the information through a little test. Ask yourself, "Is this a fact or is it a False Expectation Appearing Real?" The more you use that question, the more you'll become aware of when you are seeing the world through her F.E.A.R. filter.

Lessons in Lizard Handling

Think of your Fear Factor as a pet that needs training. How do you train a head lizard? With love and compassion. That reptile in your cranium was placed there to serve you. It doesn't take much to shrink its fearfulness down to a manageable size and keep it there. Be patient with your little gecko, it's doing the best it can. Here are a few basic training tips:

A smart way to begin is to simply observe your reptile in action. A lot of Lizard Speak is so ingrained and unconscious that you are probably not aware of it. Notice when you are afraid. Ask yourself: "Why am I fearful right now? Where did I get the information? Is this my direct experience or a False Experience Appearing Real?" Question it. Checking things out will reduce your fearfulness.

When limiting or fearful thoughts do come to mind, don't give them more importance than they justify. Talk to the reptile in your head as you would to a treasured pet, reminding that trembling reptile that the mammal is in charge now: "Don't worry. I'm going to take care of us. I know you are scared, and that's okay. I can handle this situation."

Try cutting back on your intake of the news. Since fear is an instinctual motivator, it is a primo tool in selling you the nightly spiel. For crying out loud, your reptilian brain wants to know about every shred of potential danger, even if it is 10,000 miles away. The more your lizard gloms onto information that says the world is not safe, the more voice it gets in your decision making. If a client is particularly fear-based, I often suggest that they spend one week without reading a newspaper or watching the evening news. For some news junkies, this assignment is even worse than going without chocolate (which is hard to imagine but true). The following week they are astonished at the dramatic drop in their general apprehension. Many sleep far better, as well.

> Are you giving yourself a pep talk or a poop talk?

Your reptile likes habits. It gets locked into repetitive motion, or non-motion, or repetitive thinking ("I'm a worthless loser, I'm a worthless loser, I'm a worthless loser"). But you can interrupt the pattern. Physical motion distracts the lizard and helps disconnect the reptilian automatic pattern button. Get up and move. Shift your physical location. Or you can stay seated and move or stretch something, even your ankles and toes or your face muscles.

If you are in an office environment, stand up and trot down the hall to the bathroom or go freshen your lipstick. Set an intention to have a new perspective by the time you return to your desk. Movement oxygenates your brain. And that's a good thing. Once you're in the bathroom, take in a deep breath. Look yourself in the eyes in the mirror. Give yourself a 3-minute pep talk. (You can do this silently if there are folks around.) Tell that lizard in your noggin that you are the boss. Tell yourself what you would tell a dear friend. Watch yourself come back with a fresh outlook.

Jesse's Story

Jesse woke up in a sweat one night. After months of agonizing, he finally knew that he wasn't going to marry his longtime girlfriend. It broke his heart to break her heart. He sadly shared the news.

Then the lizard began a command performance, telling him that he was a louse, that he would never be worthy of a good woman—or of anything good, for that matter. For weeks Jesse sulked and grieved, and his supervisor let him know that his work was suffering.

Jesse needed to leave aside his sadness and step up his productivity. Morning was his toughest time, so to break up his thoughts about his breakup, he volunteered to get the coffee for his team members on the mid-morning break. He short-circuited his reptilian catastrophizing and created his own Turnaround Technique—Got Java, Got Love. It felt great to do something for others. Plus, he got lots of positive strokes from his happily caffeinated coworkers.

You can take a break when you sense your lizard is getting the best of you. It only takes a few moments to shift out of the pattern it has set up. Make a positive choice. Back it up with a positive action. You-ville will be a happier place because of it!

Lizard Training Tips

Go on a news fast. Spend a week without watching, listening to, or reading the news.

Become a Lizard Whisperer. Handle your inner reptile with soothing words and a gentle touch.

To get out of the lizard loop, GET UP AND MOVE!

Rehabilitating the Reptile Game

Here's a success strategy that can help you "snap out of it"—out of negative thinking, that is—and stay focused on your successful outcome. It works wonders when you are in the midst of generalizing, catastrophizing, or lizard-izing.

1. *Center Yourself.* Take in a deep breath. Let it out. Now, breathe in serenity. Exhale the fear. Do this three times so you feel more calm.

2. *Ask for the Greatest Good.* As Mayor and chief animal trainer, ask for the insight that leads to the highest good for all concerned.

3. *Set Your Intention.* As Mayor, set your intention to dismantle your Fear Filter.

4. *Life or Death?* When you're smacked in the head with some fear from your head lizard, take a moment to check it out. Ask yourself, "Am I about to be eaten, run over, or killed?"

5. *Nope, It's Just F.E.A.R.* Chances are, the answer to that question was no. Your lizard has tricked you into believing in a False Expectation Appearing Real. Thank yourself for recognizing Lizard Speak for what it is. That's the first lesson in Lizard Obedience School.

6. *The F.E.A.R. Filter.* Now, disengage your F.E.A.R. filter. Are you generalizing? (Hint: Words like "never" and "always" are red flags that you may be generalizing.) Are you catastrophizing? (Hint: Getting lost

in fantasies about the worst possible scenario or potential sorrows and failures is a sign of catastrophizing.)

7. *Teach the Lizard.* As Mayor and master reptile trainer, you are the one who can shift the direction of your thoughts. Tell your reptilian brain: "Everything is okay. We're safe. I'm taking good care of you now. We can get through this."

8. *Speak Up.* Yep. Speak kind words—to you. I am a big believer in the power of talking to yourself. Comfort yourself and let the lizard know that the mammal is in charge now. (If people look puzzled, just tell them it's an assignment from your life coach. Or pretend that you're talking to someone on your phone.)

9. *Focus on the Fab.* After comforting yourself, focus your attention on a fabulous outcome you'd like to have.

10. *Thank Yourself.* Thank yourself for making the fabulous choice to direct yourself away from fear and toward the fab.

6

An Under-Used Four-Letter Word

The Hidden Power of _ _ _ _

I often start my coaching sessions with three simple questions: What is keeping you up at night? How does it affect the rest of your life? What do you really want instead?

Do the first two questions make you feel a bit queasy? Usually an uncomfortable silence fills the room. Fantastic! Taking a few minutes to identify what is gumming up your gears is a powerful act. That's the part of your life that needs some attention. Even a little progress in that area creates huge change across your life.

Believe it or not, there's a certain four-letter word that will help you. In fact, the area of your life that is the hardest for you to turn around is probably the one where you use this curious little word the least—and need it the most.

Hmmm . . . no, it's probably not the four-letter word you are thinking of. This word doesn't get much air time. Folks love bragging about how little of it they have in their life. (See, it's not that one.) They call it silly. Executives tout going without it like a badge of honor.

The P Word

This poor little misunderstood word and all it implies! If I had mentioned it in the title you probably would have skipped this chapter. You most likely think you are too mature to consider putting a bit more _ _ _ _ in your life. It's crazy that this little four-cylinder word has gotten such a bad rap because in fact it's a power tool for creativity and change.

So are you ready to guess? The word is: P-L-A-Y.

See, I knew it. As soon as you read the word you thought I'm just some California crackpot. Nope. Scientists like Paul MacLean are saying that play is a basic building block of learning. That means play is how we push past what we think are our limits. The moment I read about this research, I wanted to run down the street and ring everybody's doorbell: "Hey, did you know that play can help you solve your problems? This little piece of science could make your life easier in a flash!"

This Is Big, Big, Big!

Here's the scoop: There are only three key functions that separate mammals' behavior from that of reptiles. Three. That's it. One: the female mammal nurtures her infants for a very long time. Duh. This you knew. Two: mammals cry out when they are separated from the herd (some scientists think this is how speech began). We mammals are pack animals, and being lonely sucks. This too you knew.

Number three is what makes me want to run over to your house and knock on your front door, so don't miss it—and I know you won't because you're reading this chapter. The third is play. Yes. Play.

A turtle pops out of the egg and knows everything it's going to know. But a kitten needs to train its brain through play. And the more highly evolved the mammal, the more highly evolved is the play. Compared with the smartest dog on the planet, a human being has hundreds more ways to frolic. As the most evolved of all mammals (I am typing this quietly so my egotistical cat doesn't notice), we humans have taken play to its highest form—learning.

In your first five years on the planet you mastered your motor skills and accomplished a large portion of your lifetime's learning. The only way you were able to handle such a steep learning curve was by having fun. Playfulness is pleasurable. It was by fooling around that you discovered how things worked. You clowned with your food. You cavorted with the roll of toilet paper. Falling on your butt was almost as entertaining as tottering forward. Play is the most natural way to learn. It's your built-in system for expanding past the apparent confines of a problem into something new. Fun is a sassy success booster!

P-L-A-Y

"Play is the nicest thing nature ever did for us," says MacLean. Besides helping us solve problems, it helps us get close with one another. How? Goofing around promotes emotional warmth and har-

> *Are you overdrawn in the fun fund?*

mony. In *The Triune Brain in Evolution*, MacLean suggests that play evolved from the need for mom and pop mammals to bond with and educate their young. "A family that plays together stays together" isn't just a cheeseball quote from the fifties. It's a documented fact. Horsing around helped your ancestors form cohesive families. It can help you now. What is a simple way you could add some Fun Factor to a close relationship today? Try it and see.

John and Marian Bateman have one of the most joyous relationships I have ever witnessed. Marian is a leading time management consultant. John flies all over the world sharing his revolutionary Gift Work. From their heady job descriptions you might not think of them as high up on the belly laugh graph. Guess again. Just being near them makes you want to break out in a hearty giggle. It's so obvious that they are having a ball. And this is after 21 years of marriage. What's the key to their glee? Play. They relate to each other like kids. They intentionally frolic in just about every aspect of their relationship.

One weekend I was their house guest and saw it for myself. Marian was having trouble cramming everything into her suitcase, so her husband suggested she make it fun. Thus was born the Spatial Utilization Game. She was tickled at the idea of playing a game to see how effectively she could use every inch of her suitcase. Packing went from chore to creative entertainment. Later I saw them have a playful competition over who washed the dishes and who put together the vitamins for the week. They were having such a good time, I begged to join in.

Do you have a tedious chore or two that you could turn into a game? Go for it! And let me know what you come up with. I love sharing the fun.

Meeting a Master

What luck! I met a master of play the other day, a two-year-old who had volumes to teach about the power of frolicking. We played on the beach as he explored every aspect of sand. He had no preconceived notions about what was good or bad. He had just as much fun throwing sand in his own face as he did flinging it into the ocean. The play guru put the sand up to his ear expecting a symphony. At one point he got so excited, he looked at me with an "Okay, now!" and dove into the sand and swam. He did his best dog paddle. Who cared if it was in the sand? It was a blast! He was covered—sand in his undies, in his hair, all over his face, in his mouth—oh, what fun! To him, sand in his pants wasn't a problem, it was a new sensation.

> *Play can make your day.*

What lessons did the enjoyment wizard's master class in play demonstrate? He delighted in each experience with full-out joy. He took risks. He was continually doing something new. He savored every moment with spellbound curiosity. Each sensation was a delight. He saw everything afresh and with wonder.

What part of play could help you get out of your own way? If you made even one of his masterful insights your own, it could transform your day.

If you really want to amp up your problem-solving abilities, why not go observe the experts? Go down to a playground and watch kids at play. And to really get fabtized, ask a mom if you can join in the play of her two-year-old.

Problem-Solving Turbocharged

Ha! you may still be thinking. What impact is a bit of frolicking going to have on my industrial-strength problems? Play
is for toddlers and folks on vacation. My problems are serious.
My boss is querulous. My schedule makes me delirious. Why
are you wasting my time with something juvenile like this?

I'll say again: Don't underestimate the power of play as a
surefire success strategy. It's a powerful tool for dealing with the
complexities of your adult life. Brain researchers like Neil
Greenberg are suggesting that creativity—which is how we solve
problems—involves rich neurological connections between various areas of the brain. While we are born with a lot of these
connections already in place, they are further developed through
our experience, especially in the early years of life. And that's
when we're the busiest at play.

I like to imagine the state of play as a phase when the various parts of your brain, like the parts in the engine of your car,
are humming along smoothly together. If the environment becomes threatening, however, the reptilian brain slams on the
brakes and shifts you down to basic survival thinking. As you
become fearful or worried or take a victim stance, the easy access between the various parts of your brain gets short-circuited,
and you start driving around your day in first gear.

I figure that to keep up with the complications of today's
world, we need all systems on go—that is, we need to be in creative mode. Heck, I need my brain on full throttle just to figure
out my new PDA. Since play is the innate way we explore, it
jumpstarts the brain. It gets your whole brain thumping again.

Researchers are discovering that playfulness actually makes your brain more pliable and more receptive to new information. It promotes openness, spontaneity, and unpredictability, which are ingredients for maintaining a healthy brain through the years.

So, fun fosters creativity, problem solving, bonding with others, and staying young. It's a savvy strategy. Chalk one up for our team!

Because play sparks inventiveness, my personal bet is that it figured in some of the greatest advances in understanding our world. Let's take something simple, like . . . say, gravity. My brothers loved to climb up to the top of the barn and drop things off the roof. Maybe Italian guys in the late 1500s were the same. Galileo got

> *When the going gets tough, the savvy get silly.*

together with some of his buddies and said, "Hey, let's drop some stuff off the Leaning Tower of Pisa. Yeah! Some different-sized iron balls. Won't it be cool to see which one crashes first?" Thus was born the theory of gravity.

Imagine the problem solving you could awaken if you played a tad more. It would be a lot. Why? Because it's the natural way your brain learns.

Get Fresh

So how do you play with a dilemma of your own? Do you dream of making more cash but think it's impossible, do you long to be held by the one you love—even if you haven't met him yet—or do you just want a few minutes to yourself?

First: *Begin by breaking up the patterned thinking of the reptilian brain. Get Up to Get Up. Physically get up. I know I'm repeating myself . . . but have you tried it yet?*

Second: *Hand the baton to the mammalian brain: Play! Sashay down to the water cooler. Shake what your momma gave you. See how much blue you see on the way. Then spot all the red. Count all the circles. Then all the squares. Imagine which animal each of your coworkers might be in the circus. Hmmm. That was different. Play it your way. Make up your own game.*

Third: *Connect. Invite others to get involved. Play is one of the ways we bond and de-stress. Ask someone, "Will you play with this problem with me?" Then see what new ideas and opportunities show up.*

Play's Hidden Power

People ask: "What is it about your work that seems to attract opportunity?" "Where is that invisible success magnet hidden?" Indeed. How could a woman in Colorado start a PR business and be making more than she did in her corporate job after only five months? Why would a client get more job offers in two weeks than in her previous four months of job hunting? Why would the producer of *The Dr. Phil Show* call about giving this book to the studio audience of a pilot she was doing before the book was even finished? I believe the answers have to do with inviting the Great Good's

Play can help you find your way.

guidance and harnessing the overlooked power of that under-used four-letter word.

Some folks think I'm bonkers when I give them their first Fun Factor homeplay for the week. One woman asked, "I came to you to grow my business. Why on earth am I supposed to put on my favorite music and dance for 15 minutes every day?" One week later, she was seeing such an improvement in her problem-solving abilities that she was hooked on giving herself fun breaks.

Play was certainly the operative word when my own career opened up. My assistant, with some coaching help from me, had gone from answering my phones to singing for Barbra Streisand and Brad Pitt on her opening night. She had beaten out people on Broadway to land a lead in a hit show. The story was so inspiring that a TV station wanted to do a piece on how I helped her go from secretary to star. Tomorrow. Unfortunately, the telephone book of a contract she had signed to do the show wouldn't let her do any publicity. And the lawyers were refusing to budge. I was waiting for the call but it was looking hopeless, so I figured it was time to give P-L-A-Y a try.

I was in the funk and needed to find some fab. First thing: I got up. I started walking . . . okay, pacing . . . around my house. A girl's gotta do what a girl's gotta do. Next: I figured it was time to play Change Your Outfit, Change Your Outlook. I put on my Good Idea Boa. I slipped into my Tall Girl Shoes. They always make me feel more confident. I grabbed one of my trusty tiaras. What the heck.

Then: I called a PR pro and asked if she would play with some ideas. Sure, I was sweating bullets. But walking in those snazzy shoes wearing a boa and tiara helped me be more lighthearted and creative. I called other folks who knew about all the TV mumbo jumbo and invited them to take a few minutes and play. Not a single person turned me down. (Just about everyone can find five minutes to P-L-A-Y. People are starved for a bit of fun, and if you're having a blast, everybody wants to be part of it.) Creative ideas surged forth from every person I called!

No, I didn't get to do that news story. But because of all the connections I made that day, the following month I appeared on not one but two TV shows. And that lead to an incredible project with an Emmy-award-winning producer and later an opportunity to do a coaching on national television.

I firmly believe that play is magic.

Cecile's Story

In our first session Cecile let me know that what she longed for was an inner smile. She smiled so brightly for everyone else, but she longed to grin when no one was around. As with many folks, her vibrancy was being strangled by a Puritan work ethic that pooh-poohed anything nonproductive. This patrician Southern lady, now retired after a successful law career, had social obligations on top of her everyday To Do list—luncheons to organize, thank you notes to pen, and events to coordinate in connection with her advocacy work for the poor. Her nails were perfect, her hair was perfect, and underneath her gracious demeanor she was perfectly miserable.

Play was the last thing on Cecile's mind. Those muscles had atrophied long ago. Yet getting goofy was the route to help Cecile get out of the way and let her joy have a say. When she took office as the Mayor of Cecile-ville, much to my surprise, her town was a Spice Market in Istanbul. The fluorescent colors and pungent smells were a long way from the hushed tones and tastefully muted hues of the life she lived. I gave her a buffet of playful activities to try. She chose to wear lots of bracelets and walk in the park near her home—which she had never visited—in her favorite pink tennies. The jangle of bracelets reminded her of the exotic nature of Cecile-ville. It got her to the next step.

Even though she was a Neiman Marcus shopper, she tried something new. She went to the 99-cent store to buy twenty dollars worth of playthings. Just for her. Who knew? Cheap sparkly

> *Change your outfit, change your outlook.*

signs, a magic wand, and of course a tiara tickled her to the core. (Doesn't every gal need a tiara?) As she began finding small ways to bring play into her day, she started dressing in brighter colors and laughing more.

To her own amazement, having the intention to be whimsical gave her confidence in challenging situations—like meetings in Washington D.C. on behalf of the needy during a time of government cuts. Cecile made sure she packed some of her play tools, like her magic wand and ribbons to wear in her hair at the hotel. "Play kept me in the here and now. Being more lighthearted helped me to build a bridge to agency officials. And it made me more creative. It was easier to find solutions. I was astonished at how much more effective I became when I used my play skills."

Cecile even experimented with one of my most beloved

Turnaround Techniques, Wedding Gown Therapy. Her assignment one week was to buy a full-tilt gown at a consignment store and wear it around the house if she started feeling blue. (I have a selection of second-hand wedding gowns in my own closet for just this purpose.) Walking around her house in an ivory gown with turquoise shoes brought her Inner Istanbul to life. Yes, it was kooky—and she felt vibrant.

When she changed her outfit, boy, did her outlook change. The technique was so powerful that she put it to the ultimate test. For the past twenty years her family had gathered one Sunday a month at her home for a formal dinner. Cecile would madly cook while everyone sat in the living room drinking gin and tonics. This particular Sunday she invited everyone to go to her dress-up drawer and pick out a costume. Her very proper 85-year-old mother chose a boa and a hat with an explosion of feathers. Instead of polite conversation about the weather and the goings-on in town, everyone ended up in the kitchen gabbing and giggling as they cooked the meal as a team. It was such a hit that Cecile's dress-up drawer has become a whole closet and her entire family now comes together to play on a regular basis.

The Play Answer

Does a problem have you cornered? Shift into an attitude of play. Play sees new possibilities. It taps into your creativity. Heck, play is fun, so it takes the stink of stress out of the equation. Being so pleasurable, it invites you to explore. And it brings you present, because you can't really play if you're distracted.

Isn't it time you let yourself use this hidden power to amplify your success? Even if frolicking seems foreign, it isn't. Your play muscle can't wait for you to flex it. Gee, guess what comes next!

1. *Center Yourself.* Take in a deep breath. Let it out. Now, breathe in glee. Exhale heaviness. Do this three times or until you feel more lighthearted.
2. *Ask for the Greatest Good.* As Mayor, take a moment and claim your office, and ask to express your joy for the highest good of all concerned.
3. *Set Your Intention.* Set your intention to get silly and have some fun.
4. *Let's Play.* Invite yourself to let loose, be whimsical, and discover the hidden power of play. Don't worry; you can go back to being serious in a few minutes.
5. *Get Up.* As in: Stand up. As in: Get up from your computer, chair, or chaise lounge. Well done!
6. *Move.* Have you noticed how much kids tug and roll

and zip and skip? Play is active. Take a minute to "shake what your momma gave you." Yeah, baby. Move those hips. Get your backside in motion. It's harder to stay stuck when you are moving. Besides, really connecting with and moving your body is . . . fun.

7. *Play.* Once you've opened up by moving your body, check in with yourself. What is the challenge that needs a wee bit of play? Picture your Mondo Problemo. Then invite yourself to play with it. Pick it up as if it were a two-ton boulder. Toss it in the air, and let it get lighter with each toss. As it gets less weighty, see if some solutions come up.

8. *Play Some More.* What did you love to play as a kid? Was it jacks, jump rope, or swinging on the jungle gym? What is the first thing that pops up? Find some time this week to give yourself the glee of playing at your old favorite game again.

9. *Ask.* Have you noticed how much kids love to tug and roll and zip and skip *with each other*? Play with a pal. Paint flower pots, swing in swings, or get together and go to a children's store.

10. *Gee, Thanks!* Thank yourself for choosing to give yourself the freedom to express your joy.

7

What Movie Are You Starring In?

Envisioning Success

Do you say you want a better relationship with your co-worker, but the memory of her snubbing you last night keeps screeching through your head? Do you try to envision a better job in the future but keep revisiting bleak scenes of past failures instead? Like the rest of us, you may not realize that your mind's addiction to reruns is actually an incredible tool for creating more fabulousity—once you know how to use it. As Mayor, you have the clout to leverage one of your most powerful resources—the You-ville movie industry. Yep, you can decide what's playing on the silver screen in your head. And a fast way to leave your blues behind is to focus on the positive. The more you direct yourself to win in your own fantasies, the happier your life will be. Yes, my cupcake, choosing what head movie you're screening is a powerful way to shift out of funk and into more fabulousness.

Film Festival

Think of it as a film festival that's playing 24/7 in You-ville.

Spotlights scan the night sky. Paparazzi gather near the entrance. Every polished toenail in You-ville is ready to feel the touch of the red carpet. It's the place to be. This is where your future begins.

The You-ville Film Festival makes the kind of impact every movie star and studio mogul goes to bed at night dreaming about. Every single film you feature doesn't just change the world . . . it actually creates the reality you live in.

Why is it so powerful? Scientists have found that the brain cannot tell the difference between reality and a well-imagined fantasy. Pictures either propel or repel you. Whatever you put in the projector of your inner screening room makes a powerful statement about how you want your life to be. As you picture yourself enjoying more health, wealth, and happiness, you are moving toward making those images reality.

> *Pictures either propel or repel you.*

Leading athletes have been using this technique for decades. They spend hours a day sitting in chairs imagining themselves performing at the top of their game. As a competition nears, Olympic skiers actually spend more time visualizing themselves doing a perfect run than physically training. The secret to being a top athlete isn't a matter of muscle, it's a matter of positive focus.

So What's Playing?

So, my friend, what film is running in that mind of yours? If I bought a ticket to what's currently showing . . . would it be a horror flick rerun of how bad your last date was? A dreary propaganda film about all the stuff you should be doing and aren't?

A slapstick romantic comedy with you having all the great costumes, the great lines, and getting the great guy? Every day you are starring in the movie of your mind. Why not make it a fabulish one?

Often when I ask clients to picture themselves with their dreams coming true, they start telling me all the reasons it will never happen. Instead of describing a picture of success, they explain how they're stuck. That lets me know what the cinema in their head looks like. Remember, what you focus on grows. If you wonder why you're paralyzed, or just not moving forward as fast as you'd like, maybe it's time to check out the You-ville movie listings.

Think of something you dream about having. Pick the first thing that pops into your mind. Is it a great relationship, a better job, a healthier body, a new home, more time to enjoy your friends and family?

Take a still shot from your movie and study it. What does it look like? Is it a sizzling Technicolor image of you savoring your dreams? Are you giddy with happy bubbles when you see this little pic? Is it a photo from a dream that was in vibrant color a long time ago, but years of disappointments have leached the color out of the picture? Is it a drab sepia print, tattered around the edges because you've forgotten about it, hard to look at because long ago you decided it was impossible to achieve?

Technicolor or Black and White?

I know what it's like to have the color fade from your dreams. Dragging myself to a job I hated—and also sucked at (selling custom-made shirts to smug men)—after I lost my company felt like living right next door to hell. I had lost just about everything. I was a loser. Every sparkling hope I had held for myself seemed tarnished. My heart goes out when I see that look of desperation in someone else's eyes. I know what it is like to give up on yourself. It's one of the reasons I wrote this book. I had so wished for someone to give me hope when I thought the good times in my life were over.

> *Has disappointment leached the Technicolor pigment out of your dreams?*

If you're from Kansas like I am, you hear quite a bit about Dorothy. Just like in the *Wizard of Oz,* you *can* leave the black-and-white world of disillusionment and allow the dazzling color of your dreams back into your life. It takes more than clicking your heels. But you can do it.

Let Your Dreams Have Their Say

"Build it and they will come" sums up the power of positive visualization. *Field of Dreams* is one of my favorite flicks. Iowa farmer Ray Kinsella (Kevin Costner) is inspired by a voice and vision he can't ignore. He pursues what surely seems like an insane odyssey: building a baseball field in his corn field for an imaginary game between long-dead players. Sure, he looks like a nut job to his neighbors, but he follows his inner vision anyway—and gets more than he dreamed of.

> *Why not win in your own fantasy?*

I have watched *Field of Dreams* scenarios unfold time and

time again for my clients and myself. "Get out of the way and let your dreams have their say" is so important that I have it on my business card. Once you create an inner blockbuster of success, and then take small steps to put it into production, the results are remarkable.

I have witnessed people triple their income, quit smoking, release unwanted weight, find the career of their dreams, and begin dating after years of going to the movies solo using this Turnaround Technique. You can too. I am here to testify . . . this stuff works!

Today on *The Today Show*

Two weeks ago I had such a crazy lights-camera-action experience, I have to share it with you. I was in New York City and it was a glorious day, so I walked from my hotel to the advertising agency where I had a coaching meeting. On the way, I passed the Rockefeller Center, where they film *The Today Show*. Oh, *The Today Show!* Being on *The Today Show* has always been a dream. So I took a moment and stood in Rockefeller Plaza and visualized myself on the show. I imagined myself feeling comfortable and enthusiastic. I pictured the lens of the camera. I felt myself having a great time. I heard the producer telling me it was a terrific interview. Making my mini movie took under two minutes. Off I went to my meeting on Madison Avenue.

As I began the walk back to my hotel, my GPS said, "Don't walk home the way you came. Walk back on 5th Avenue." (I've been listening to my GPS long enough that I often get pretty clear instructions.)

I turned onto 5th Avenue—whaddyaknow, there was a camera crew. "We're from *The Today Show*. Can we interview you about women and shoes?" Shoes! Are you kidding? Everyone knows that I can have a shoegasm just trying on a sexy pair of stilettos. I gurgled about how happy shoes make a happy girl. How I would be a depressed person if I didn't get my shoe fix. How I would eat peanut butter to be able to buy a great pair of shoes. Just two hours after I made my mini movie, there it was, happening for real. A few days later when they turned on their TV sets and saw me on *The Today Show,* all of America would know that I am willing to endure a peanut butter diet to increase the good shoe ratio in my closet. It was just as I had imagined it. I had a blast. The producer said, "Wow, you have amazing energy. You gave a rocking interview."

The vibrant visualization of a successful outcome gave a clear map to Me-ville. My GPS system got the heads-up and was on the lookout for the opportunity. Listening to my GPS got me to the right place at the right time. And since I had seen myself having fun being filmed, having a great time with the camera and crew was a cinch.

Let's Make a Movie!

Now it's your turn. Let's make a movie! Start by seeing yourself a year from today. (For some reason, placing your success movie in the future opens up your visioning capacities.) Now, imagine that your Fairy Godmother has waved her wand and you are watching yourself living your

If you can see it, you can be it.

most heartfelt dream. Pick a specific scene that is a highlight of that vision. Relax and enjoy the luscious delight of your success playing on the big screen of your mind. Let's say your goal is to waltz through your life with greater health and vitality in a lean, toned body.

Get a close-up on your Success Scene. That will help it spring to life. Zoom in on all your senses. What are you seeing and hearing? What are the smells, tastes, touch sensations? What are you wearing (always a key question), and how does it feel on your skin? Are you feeling your muscles tone up as you take more hikes? Do all the veggies you're eating taste sweet on your tongue? Can you feel the sun on your skin as you lie in a swimsuit by the pool? Are you hearing your skinny jeans zip up with ease? Where are you? Who is with you? Remember, the brain is unable to tell the difference between an actual fact and a well-imagined fantasy.

The Union of Emotions can help you sell a lot of tickets, so don't forget to make a movie they love. The Mental Board is terrific in helping develop the details of your Success Scene. Inviting your GPS to give suggestions or input is a smart idea. Its greater

> *Lights. Camera. Now take an action.*

perspective and tie-in to whatever is the highest good for all concerned may give you the courage to go for something you would otherwise write off as impossible. Amazing magic can happen when all of You-ville is behind your project.

Once you have visualized your Success Scene, capture it in a Success Script. Write it down. Numerous studies have shown that writing down a goal makes it far more likely to occur.

Now you have two versions of your Success Movie to work with: the visualized scene and the written screenplay. Every You-ville is set up a little differently. If you love images and color, you can watch the Success Scene. If it's easier for you to engage with your success while reading about it, read the Success Script out loud. If you are a person who absorbs information more easily through hearing, you may want to record yourself reading the script and then listen to it.

The more often you visualize, read, or hear about your Success Movie, the more alive and real it becomes for your brain. It gets used to the idea of you, say, at your ideal weight or in your ideal job or with your ideal man.

Finally, start taking the steps to make your Success Scene happen. Ask yourself, "What action can I take today to make my movie a reality?" Making a phone call, Googling a resource, or brainstorming a plan can take under 15 minutes and can bring you one step closer to manifesting your success. (It's sure how this book came into being.) Being clear on your goal helps you see the small steps that will get you there. Once you start taking those steps, you will be amazed and delighted at how quickly you move forward.

Secrets to a Huge Blockbuster

Here are some trade secrets to making your movie a box-office smash in You-ville:

Make it at least 50 percent believable:

Let's say you are dreaming of buying a home. If your Create

Your Reality Festival runs the film "Look, Mom, I Bought a Multi-Million Dollar Mansion," your Mental Board may scoff. They have the rational data to prove that your flick is total fiction. But if you show "Fab House—The True Story of How I Bought a Home I Love, Love, Love," your Mental Board members will line right up for tickets. And as they view the picture over and over, they will start coming up with brilliant ideas of how to make it happen.

Juicy, juicy, juicy:

Make it colorful, gleeful, and fab-tastic. Fill the script with oodles of adverbs and adjectives. As director of your Success Film, you want to make your vision as yummy and dramatic as possible. Which would grab a bigger audience: "I am going to buy a house," or "I am sitting in the breakfast room savoring my hot Earl Grey tea and the quiet of the Saturday morning. I feel embraced by my home, and its beauty inspires me. I am so content and relaxed as I hear the birds singing. What a delight to relish the morning! Looking out through the huge windows I see a hummingbird zoom past the peonies growing along the deck. I am so grateful"?

Make the movie in the now:

Use present tense verbs in your script. See yourself being, having, and doing what you want in your scene. (A movie, even one set in the future, is always happening now when it is playing.) If you tell yourself that you will buy a house, you reinforce the idea that owning a house is always out ahead of you in the future. You never see yourself actually enjoying ownership of a house.

Details, details, details:

You make your movie come alive by coloring in all the particulars. Whether it's your turquoise sandals, running on the beach in a baseball cap and a bikini, or looking at the bouquet of flowers from your favorite florist, it's the details that enliven your script. What quirky fine points make your Success Script leap with life?

Mine reads something like this: I am filled with a warm glow of gratitude for my lean, strong, vibrantly healthy, beautiful body. Hot diggity dog, I am celebrating how great I feel having more energy than when I was in my twenties. Wow, I am overflowing with loving and gratitude for all the good in my life. What fun! I loving glancing in the mirror and seeing that my skinny jeans are baggy. "Gosh, Eli, you just don't seem to age. You just keep getting better" is a phrase I love hearing. Yum. Since I am honoring myself, it's natural for me to choose healthy foods. I am relishing how great I feel as I savor all the creative, fun ways I get my exercise. It's a delight to smell the flowers and drink in the beauty of nature as I take my walks. Wow, I am feeling my strength and my flexibility as I move through my day. I am delighted to be honoring my Alliance of Body Parts. Each cell of my body is filled with gratitude to the Great Good.

Loren's Story

Loren's spirit was a blaze of vibrant colors hidden behind the button-down shirts she wore to her corporate marketing job.

Every cell in her body longed to express her kooky brilliance. She kept thinking about starting, of all things, her own handbag company. But she knew it wouldn't generate enough money for her to quit her job for another year or two.

I introduced her to the concept of constructing a Success Scene and let her know that she could imagine herself owning her own successful company even if she hadn't yet settled on what industry she wanted to be in. Why wait two years? I asked. Visualizing her success would help her develop a plan to get there. That idea won the lottery in Her-ville. Loren's heart wasn't set on selling handbags. She already knew lots of people working in the media—why not start a PR company? There would be little capital outlay, and she adored schmoozing with media folks.

Everything in Loren lit up. Those bright colors started glowing. She crafted a Success Scene that made her explode with delight. Her emotions erupted with enthusiasm when she described herself wearing her favorite mauve boots in her exposed brick office. She soared with joy as she visualized herself making mega moolah, enjoying her day, and achieving wild, rocking success with lightning speed.

Within one week of crafting "The Movie of My Smashing Success," Loren had her first client. Within four months, she had seven clients. At month five (I was biting my nails that it was far too soon) she went to the powers that be at the corporation she worked for. She had made a new Success Script of how her current employer would love to become a PR client. Loren let her bosses know she had started her own public relations company and suggested that they hire her. They said yes. Within five months of starting her own business, Loren was making more money than she had at her corporate job. She had put a stop to her stifling nine-to-fiver, her former employer had become her client, and she had begun living the life of her dreams. That's five months, folks.

The Success Script Game

You are the writer, director, producer, and star of what's showing in your Fabulous Success Film Festival. The more often you view it, the better. The more detail you add, the better. The juicer it is, the better.

1. *Center Yourself.* Actors do concentration exercises and warm up their "instrument" before performing. You can too. As you focus on your breathing, stretch your body. Breath in clarity. Breath out confusion and doubt.

2. *Ask for the Greatest Good.* As Mayor, take a moment and ask for inspiration that aligns with the highest good for all.

3. *Set Your Intention.* Set your intention to allow your authentic success to be expressed.

4. *It's a Smash.* Hold a You-ville Town Meeting. Ask your neighborhoods to assist you in creating a terrific Success Scene. If you like having a Fairy Godmother, bring her in too! Pick a goal that gets everyone excited and be sure it's at least 50 percent believable.

5. *See Yourself.* It's one year from today. See yourself rollicking and frolicking in your Success Scene. Just like the Olympic athletes do, create a specific scene where you see yourself enjoying your accomplishment. Make sure you see yourself having a blast.

6. *Sense Yourself.* Use your other senses to build the de-

tail. Leading with other senses may be even more powerful than making seeing the primary sense. What are you hearing, touching, tasting, smelling? What emotions are you feeling? Explore with your ears. Sniff out the smells. Take your emotional temperature. Each sense you add makes the scene more realistic. Great!

7. *Draft Your Script.* Write down your Success Scene and make it into your Success Script. Describe the action as if it is happening right now. Be realistic and specific. Use present tense verbs that end in *-ing*. Add juicy adjectives and adverbs for the pop and sizzle.

8. *Get Involved.* Review your Success Scene. Play the movie of your success frequently. Post playbills all over You-ville. Record yourself reading your Success Script and listen to it before you go to bed. Read your Success Script every morning as you drink your coffee. The more often you review your Success Scene, the more natural your belief in your success becomes.

9. *Go into Production.* Put your Success Script into action. Take small steps toward your success.

10. *Thank Yourself.* Thank yourself for choosing to direct your life's energy.

8

Overcoming Perfectionitis

Lighten Up

Do you set up a Success Scene Strategy only to find yourself procrastinating when it comes to taking action? Do you look at your dream and feel that you don't quite measure up? Is your inner nag always finding something to pick apart about your projects? Don't worry, you aren't alone. You probably have a case of the latest bug going around, a debilitating condition known as Perfectionitis.

How can wanting to "be the best you can be" be a disease? Sorry. It's a trap. That's why this disorder is so troubling. You just want to do a perfect job, be a perfect person. Sure. Point well taken. The only problem is . . . there ain't no such thing as perfection. Excellence, yes. Perfection, no. Perfection is a fantasy, and unfortunately most Americans have bought into it.

Holey moley, I may be out on a limb here, but I am proposing that Perfectionitis is a modern-day epidemic—that it falls in the category of ailment rather than annoyance. And the good folks at Webster's are ready to back up my thesis. Here are a few handy definitions:

Disease: *a condition of the living animal or plant body or one of its parts that impairs normal functioning and is typically manifested by distinguishing signs and symptoms.*

Perfect: *being entirely without fault or defect; corresponding to an ideal standard or abstract concept; the excellence of every part, element, or quality of a thing frequently as an unattainable or theoretical state <a* perfect set of teeth>.

Perfection: *flawlessness; the quality or state of being saintly.*

-itis: *a suffix used in pathological terms that denote inflammation of an organ* (bronchitis, gastritis, neuritis) *and hence, in extended senses, nouns denoting abnormal states or conditions, excesses, tendencies, obsessions, etc.*

There you have it. Does an inflamed obsession to achieve an abstract standard of saintly flawlessness in every part, element, and quality of you sound familiar? You impair your normal state— the healthy, joyous expression of the true you—and impair your life when you try to push yourself to be perfect. Just like any ailment, perfectionism is destructive and it needs treatment.

Perfectionitis: What the Heck Is It?

Perfectionitis is what happens when your internal "should" muscle becomes inflamed. It shifts you into an abnormal state, a crazy condition of self-sabotaging thoughts and behaviors that makes you hurl yourself toward unrealistic goals. If you have a case of Perfectionitis, your You-ville Criticism Committee has gone berserk. They have flipped into a perpetual carp that you could look, do, and be . . . better. I know. I have a pretty good case of it myself. I once caught myself criticizing myself for the way I opened a door. Jeez.

You try to shut down the Crit Com by proving how really, really super good you are. You are determined to be flawless. Unfortunately, it's impossible to convince the panel of judges sitting on your inner Committee. (They know your flaws all too well. Like how those unreturned DVDs are still on the back seat of your car, how you fudged your last sick day, and that you have a secret crush on your neighbor's husband.) So instead you long to impress other people so they'll give you positive strokes. Looking good to others becomes a salve to soothe the harshness of what goes on in your head.

Signs and Symptoms: The Overs

Perfectionitis pushes you into the Overs. Overs? Yep. Overachieve: you can never be ordinary, you need a consummate success. Overload: you pile three days' worth of stuff into one day's schedule. Overkill: instead of simply doing your best, you obsess on doing every minute detail impeccably. Overwhelm: you feel defeated because you can never complete the endless tasks you set for yourself.

> *Feel over the edge? Check the Overs: Overachieve. Overload. Overkill. Overwhelm.*

Strange as it seems, Perfectionitis also sets you up for procrastination. Why? Some people are paralyzed by not wanting to make a mistake, get it wrong, look stupid, or, heaven forbid . . . fail. You postpone starting because you don't want to risk not

Telltale Indications:
How the Heck Can I Tell If I Have It?

Here are some handy questions to ask yourself to see if you have a touch of Perfectionitis:

Do you feel driven to look good in others' eyes or to get approval from them?

Are you usually trying to accomplish several huge goals at the same time?

Do you rarely finish everything you have planned for yourself in a given day?

Are you unforgiving of your own funky parts?

Are you unforgiving of the flaws of others?

Do you procrastinate when you start a project because you are afraid you won't do it well enough?

Do you obsess over doing something flawlessly to the point of ignoring your needs?

Do you doubt your own decisions?

Do you say yes when you mean no?

Do you make your fun time or free time into a job?

Do you feel like you are never doing enough?

Do you think you have to do it all yourself?

If you said yes to three or more of these, you may have caught the bug.

meeting your own impossibly high standards. If you can never do it well enough, why do it anyway?

Sometimes Perfectionitis settles in one particular part of your life—work or cleaning or exercise or shopping or volunteering (whatever is your perfectionism of choice). But other parts of your life suffer because you are pretty dang . . . well, obsessive about that

> *Perfectionism leads to procrastination, paralysis, and panic.*

one part and don't give the rest enough attention. Any way you look at it, Perfectionitis louses up your life.

Lacey's Story

Lacey is a sleek and fastidious fashion designer with a very severe case of Perfectionitis. No one can live up to her high expectations, not even her childhood best friend, Kimberly. After years of living in different cities, she and Kim decided to get an apartment together in San Francisco. Even though Lacey adores her friend, she would sob on the way home. She couldn't bear to be in the apartment. She wanted to scream every time she found Kim's teacups on the coffee table and her running shoes in the dining room. Lacey's image of herself as someone who never showed a negative emotion kept her from discussing the issue with Kim. She told herself that she didn't want to hurt Kim's feelings. Her inner rant grew and her outer iciness increased. She moved out, saying she needed to live closer to the office. But teacups and tennis shoes were the real reason. She and Kim drifted apart.

Lacey's Perfectionitis seems to find just about everyone an

irritant, so she lives a quiet and desperately lonely life. Guys don't measure up, and she considers her family a mess. Christmas, Thanksgiving, and pretty much every holiday Lacey spends by herself because she thinks nobody else cooks well enough.

Demographics: Who the Heck Gets It?

Just about everybody these days seems to have one or two Perfectionitis symptoms. I don't see a lot of people who are living in healthy self-acceptance. The culture just doesn't support it. As a woman, you are likely to have the added pressure of managing both work and home life. If you are an entrepreneur like me, you are trying to do everything. If you are a woman working in a corporate environment, you may have to work harder than the men to prove yourself. Basically, if you own a bra and have ever worn pantyhose, my money is on the table that you have a touch of the old Perfectionitis bug.

Our society, founded on the Protestant work ethic, seems to think the Impossible Workload is just peachy keen and even necessary for success. People get more strokes for achievement than for being happy, so they willingly take on what is in fact a toxic work schedule. Magazines are full of stories of super women who cook as well as Martha Stewart, are as slim as Kate Moss, run an empire like Oprah, and claim to have a dreamy marriage, all on three hours of sleep a night. News journals sing the praises of executives who hardly rest like they're a new, improved breed of capitalist warrior, above and beyond the

Pop quiz:
Is it better to be successful or
happy? Happy = Successful.

mere mortal who needs a daily eight hours of shut-eye and eight glasses of water. "Extreme Jobs (and the People Who Love Them). 80-Hour Weeks? Endless Travel? High Stress? Bring It On!" was the cover caption on an edition of *Fast Company* magazine. Next to the article was a cartoon of a woman holding a cell phone: "I Have No Life . . . and I Love It!" Boy, she sure needs an anti-Perfectionitis prescription!

Lydia's Story

More and more companies are demanding insane work loads as a norm. A member of an audience of women executives I spoke to drove the point home dramatically. Lydia is a slim, vibrant brunette with bright eyes. A partner in a large law firm, she was about to retire. After the talk, she shared with me: "In the late seventies and early eighties the hours I put in made me look like one of the hardest-working people in the firm. If I worked those same hours as a young lawyer who had just joined the firm today, I would be fired as a slacker." Her voice lowered as she continued. "My daughter is a young attorney who is trying to become a partner at a law office in New York City. She works such long hours that the stores are closed by the time she goes home. Sometimes she doesn't even have time to go buy toilet paper, so she steals some from the firm's supply."

Etiology: How the Heck Does It Happen?

Two things come together to bring on a bout of Perfectionitis: a culture that values high performance above everything else, and a person with low self-esteem who has assimilated those values and is motivated to try to live up to them. When you believe somewhere inside that you are unworthy, inadequate, or incompetent, it's easy to start living from the outside in. You do things to get approval from others—the culture, your boss, family, teacher, colleagues, or children—instead of doing what is a healthy choice for you.

As a kid it is easy to equate being good with being loved. Your good manners get applauded. The bad ones are punished. As time goes on, your value as a person may seem to be based on how you perform. In some families there is even the message that if you don't excel at school, sports, or socially, you are a big failure. Behavior, then, appears to be a magic wand. It has the power to get you more love. How intoxicating! It casts its spell time and time again.

If you were like me growing up, you thought, "Boy, I want to be loved all of the time, but I can't be good all of the time. I can only be good some of the time. If I can't be good all the time, I must be bad inside. That means I have to work extra hard to do things really, really, really well."

Like so many other women, you become a champion self-nitpicker. You chide yourself about your weight, your career, your woefully single status. Self-criticism is a convoluted defense mechanism: "If I am hard on myself, then other people won't have to be."

Amanda's Story

Amanda's father was a busy executive running a successful

manufacturing company. He traveled frequently. Dad expected good grades, good looks, and good behavior from each of his five children. Since there was a very limited quantity of Dad in her life, Amanda was determined to have his attention when he was around. She figured that if she could prove herself extraordinary at school and on the tennis court, she could earn some face time. Amanda was honors everything in high school. She was All-State in tennis.

Her Dad congratulated her successes, but believing that she needed to earn his recognition left Amanda feeling empty. Unconsciously she decided to "show" her father by becoming even more successful than he was. Amanda put the pedal to the metal and climbed the Fortune 500 ladder as a corporate attorney. Soon she had the McMansion in the fancy neighborhood and the eighty-hour work week to maintain her lifestyle. No matter how tired she was, she managed to make herself get in a workout to keep her figure flawless. Some mornings she would almost vomit from exhaustion, but she would go to the gym anyway. Amanda started drinking as a way to "come down" from the day. Soon she kept a small bottle at her desk to "keep her sane." Her lunch hour became lush hour. Later that year she was fired when she fell asleep, drunk, in the middle of a long trial.

Life in the Less Than Perfect Lane

What would life be like without the disease? (Yep, it is possible to live that way!) The opposite of Perfectionitis is what researchers call "healthy striving." Studies show that healthy strivers set realistic goals that are the natural next step from where they are now. You can too! Go ahead and dream big. Then lay out a set of reasonable steps that will get you there. That way you can work smarter, not harder.

Not only that. You get to acknowledge yourself for completing each step along the way. That adds up to a lot of positive internal reinforcement. The more steps you get to declare done and done well, the more you build your self-image as someone savvy and successful. And that feels great. Instead of rewarding yourself only when you reach the mondo outcome, you savor the delights of the journey. Since it's a pretty fab expedition, you take the flubs and toe stubs into account as part of the adventure.

There are no perfect people. Everyone has zits or cellulite or both.

Healthy striving goes along with healthy self-esteem. And when your self-esteem is alive and well, you tend to live from the inside out. You "pick a game you can win," as my pal Kathryn Allen says. You go for things that have juice for you inside and are attainable outside. You pay attention to the smarts inside of you. As Mayor, you hold regular Town Meetings so your destination is somewhere everyone in You-ville wants to go. You let go of the Shoulds and let the dreams of your heart have a say. When you do, you can't help but take better care of you. And, miracle of miracles, you cut yourself some slack, and others too.

Sounds like the perfect way to live? Are you beating yourself up because these three paragraphs don't seem to describe you? Watch out. Perfectionitis may be infecting the way you read this. It's easy to be a perfectionist about not having Perfectionitis! But there's an antidote. Read on.

The good news is that no one is unblemished. As far as I can tell, there isn't a single perfect person on the planet. Everyone has zits or cellulite or both. Everyone gets angry and disappointed. There isn't a person around that doesn't have some weird quirk or secret they'd probably prefer to keep to themselves. Hallelujah! Those vulnerabilities are what make each of us unique and even more lovable.

Who would want to live in a world of Stepford Wives? Not me. So why not give yourself a little break today? Let whatever isn't as good as you want it to be, be okay. Take a few minutes to let yourself just be. Be fab. Just as you are.

Treatment: The Get a Life Game

Now it's time to kick off your Perfectionitis treatment plan.

1. *Center Yourself.* Take in three deep breaths of tenderness. Let out three deep breaths of fatigue. Brava! You just took a step toward replenishing yourself. Way to go!
2. *Ask for the Greater Good.* As Mayor, take a moment and claim your office, and ask that your choices are aligned with the highest good for all concerned.
3. *Set Your Intention.* Set the intention to be gentle with yourself and to honor all of you.
4. *Just Say No.* Take a look at what's on your schedule. Write down what you plan to get done today. How much time have you marked out for each item?

Double it. Stuff takes longer than you think. What items on your list can be removed? Say no to those tasks and renegotiate their timeline. Dr. Andrew Jacobs, one of the country's top sports psychologists, has helped Olympic champions cultivate the mental attitudes that make them winners. He suggests to his clients, "Learn to say no. Learn to let go."

5. *Get Real.* That's not all. Where is your You Time? If you don't schedule in time for yourself, who will? As Mayor, plan a recess break of at least 15 minutes. And make sure you keep it.

6. *Get Really Real.* Take a peep at your To Do list. Are your goals realistic? Or would you need to clone yourself to get everything done? Take a tip from my friend David Allen. Make a Maybe Someday list of those items you'd like to get to but can't at the moment. Check your Maybe Someday list weekly to see if the status has changed.

7. *Get Really, Really Real.* Stop being the Lone Ranger. Pick up the phone. Ask for help or advice. You probably have a pal who excels in an area that isn't your best.

8. *Keep It Real.* Sharing support is a sure sign of being in Perfectionitis recovery. There's nothing like pairing up with somebody to help you get real. Check in with each other. Having a buddy helps you to keep your commitment to take care of you while setting more realistic goals.

9. *Praise and Prize.* Congratulate yourself often. Even for the silly little things. "Boy, what a good job of flossing I did today." "Bravo, that was a superb meal I prepared for the cat." The more you praise yourself, the less you will be driven to seek praise from others.

10. *Play.* Don't forget to focus on FUN! You have the working-hard stuff down.

11. *Thank Yourself.* Thank yourself for making a fabulous choice to take back your life.

9

Are You Baking Brownies or Burning "Blackies"?

Take Good Care of Yourself

Women are genetically designed to give, give, and give. Consider this little factoid about the female human body: If a pregnant woman isn't getting enough calcium in her diet, her body leaches the calcium out of her bones to feed her baby. An expectant mom takes calcium supplements precisely for this reason—her cells are ready to put her baby's health before her own.

Our biochemistry comes fully loaded to make this kind of mind-boggling self-sacrifice. Maybe that's why so many women take selfless generosity for granted. We forget that "giving until it hurts" is intended only for real emergencies. Even if you don't have kids, you probably find yourself aiding coworkers, neighbors, those in your congregation, or those less fortunate. You see a need and jump in, just like the calcium in your bones. Thank goodness. Giving is a blessing. But overgiving (giving while ignoring your own requirements) turns that gift into a burden.

Hello. Wake up and smell the coffee. Since you're programmed to put others first, choosing to take care of yourself may feel backward. C'mon, baby doll: Do it anyway.

Betty Crocker or Betty's Off Her Rocker?

When a woman—let's call her Betty—ignores her needs (for sleep or intimacy or exercise or whatever else keeps her purring), she's eventually going to turn herself into toast.

She is trying to look like the new-millennium poster girl: the perfectly decorated home, the great kids, the flourishing career, the happy marriage. From across the street she looks like Betty Crocker Superwoman. She dashes home from a demanding job and pops a batch of brownies in the oven before speeding a minivan full of kids off to soccer practice. The neighbors across the street smell the aroma of fresh-baked goods wafting on the air and wonder, "How does she do it?"

But up close you can see that Betty's Off Her Rocker. If she isn't taking some time for herself, she is barreling down the road to disaster. If those neighbors walked into her kitchen, they'd see she was scorching a batch of "blackies." Betty's so frazzled she doesn't even notice the alarm blaring in her smoke-filled kitchen. Or that she's offering her family and friends delicious little bits . . . of blackened carbon. But she is.

Put yourself last, and there's gonna be a big ol' mess to clean up.

Sure, she may look great—for a while. But if she's overlooking her own needs, Betty's gonna get bitter and start hitting the bottle, pounding on the bakery counter, or collapsing in a puddle of exhaustion. And once the smoke clears, she has years of grimy residue all over her kitchen cabinets to clean up.

That's what comes from putting herself last. Ugh, all that scrubbing on top of everything else! Even Betty Crocker isn't exempt from paying the price for pushing past her boundaries.

Nicole's Story

Friends shook their heads and wondered how Nicole did it. She was the major breadwinner in her family, with three small children. Her husband, Frank, was an inventor. His projects never seemed to make any money, but they took him out of town continually. On top of making most of the money and doing most of the parenting, Nicole was the backbone of her church volunteer program. She even wrote children's books "on the side." If someone in the community was in need, they'd turn to Nicole first. And she never said no. She would stay up until three in the morning making care baskets for a battered women's shelter even if she had a deadline at work. Many thought she should be sainted. Except for the staff at her church, who secretly resented her for making them look like deadbeats.

Nicole always claimed that she never needed much sleep. Until she did. Her years of baking "blackies" caught up with her. Even during a difficult pregnancy she continued to work grueling hours. She had burnt herself to such a brittle fragment of her former self that she was in bed for almost a year. When she tells the story, her voice wobbles as she describes being too weak to lift her young daughter. Now Nicole is impassioned about making sure women are taking care of themselves. She leads workshops teaching self-nurturing skills to other women.

I Give Therefore I Am

You think you don't give to others first? Close your eyes. Remember how your shoulders felt on, say, December 26. Was "Surviving Christmas" (or Hanukkah or Kwanzaa or Ramadan) the subtitle to your holiday? Join the club. Around Thanksgiving time you can see the crazed caretaker component of a woman's brain kick into full gear. It sends her careening down the road to make the holidays special, honking at anyone who gets in its way right up to New Year's.

I grew up wondering why I was seeing the men lollygagging around the table and TV and the ladies laboring in the kitchen. I'm still wondering today. The woman of the house scurries around making, serving, and cleaning up after the feast for her clan. Oh, right. That is after she has trudged through the mall and shopped for, wrapped, and sent a mound of gifts. Oh, right. That is after she came home from the office and helped the kids with their homework. Oh, right. That is after she did the laundry, grocery shopping, and the housework. Oh, right. That's after she made her legendary Cinnamon Cake. Sounds crazy? I wonder what another species would say?

Burnt to a Crisp

"All I want for Christmas . . . is a nap!" was a card I couldn't resist at the local stationery store. No kidding. A lot of people are so pooped that they wonder if there's life before coffee. Look at the number of caffeine emporiums in your neighborhood and you'll get a pretty good idea of how tired everybody is. Java used to be a breakfast beverage, now it's a major food group. People must be really pooped in Seattle. They have espresso bars next to the baggage claim carousel at the airport.

Why this sudden urge for caffeine? Times have changed—probably no surprise to you. Nowadays, you need your java jolt. Americans

Are you so busy that . . . oh, right . . . you forgot to have a life?

are working harder and longer than they used to, more than any other industrialized nation (we took that title away from Japan in 1995). Each year, we work one month longer than the Japanese and three months longer than the Germans.

I was horrified a few years ago to learn a new word. *Karoshi* is Japanese for "death from overwork." Unfortunately that term has become so well-known on this side of the Pacific that it's showing up in English dictionaries. Even more tragically, it's more than just a word. I have consulted in two different companies where one day someone came to work in a Ford and went home in a body bag.

Taking care of yourself is not just a nice idea, it's essential to your survival.

When did coffee become a major food group?

I believe the epidemic of working longer and harder and not getting enough rest is particularly tough on women. It is not just that our cells are genetically engineered to give to others. Women have one-seventh of the testosterone production that men have. So what? Testosterone is a key element in muscle development, drive, and endurance. And endurance is what you need for the insanely long hours you're putting in.

Women drive themselves as hard if not harder than their male colleagues in the office because as a sex we are newer in the work-

Do you have to flambé your day?

place. Yet, in my opinion, we don't have the testosterone reserves to support that pace. If you add parenting to the mix, you have the perfect recipe for a big batch of "blackies." Your body needs some down time. If you need an excuse, tell yourself and your loved ones that you are doing it for the sake of your health.

When the Going Gets Tough, the Tough Get Horizontal

The first place to start replenishing yourself might just be under the covers. Even though you may be working harder than ever, you're probably sleeping less. America has a hidden debt that is growing every year. We suffer from what researchers are calling "sleep debt." The United States is a sleep-deprived country. More and more scientific data is indicating that you and I aren't getting the shut-eye we need. Seven out of every ten Americans is getting seven hours or less of sleep. Yet other studies show that eight hours of sleep is as important as a good diet and exercise. Why? During sleep is

Pay down your debt without touching your check book. Get some extra zzzzz's.

when your body recovers and regenerates after the wear and tear of your day.

It's no big surprise that you function better after enough zzzzz's. You know how tired you are after a sleepless night. You're feeling the effects of not getting the renewal you needed. Your ability to focus and make decisions goes down by a whopping 50 percent. Your communication skills slide by 30 percent, and your memory by 20 percent, says Mark Rosekind, board member of the National Sleep Foundation as well as president and chief scientist at Alertness Solutions.

To make matters worse, having a large sleep debt mimics the signs of aging. They don't call it Beauty Rest for nothing. Going with less than your eight hours of snooze time increases the risk and severity of age-related ailments like diabetes, hypertension, obesity, and memory loss—not to mention it louses up your looks.

And that doesn't even take the Crabby Factor into account. Not getting your forty winks makes you one sour puss. Studies of the brain show that you're more than twice as likely to snap at a colleague or a loved one when you haven't had enough sleep. Everyone in your life may say thank you when you take a bit more time for sweet dreams! So give yourself an extra half hour of sleep at least one night this week.

> *They don't call it Beauty Rest for nothing.*

Add Some Happiance to Your Brownie Batter

Are you thinking: But I don't have time to take time for myself? That's a bunch of hooey from your I-give-therefore-I-am genes. Sure you're swamped, but as Mayor you can decide to wedge some small but succulent treats into your day. Have you noticed that a few bites of a French chocolate are more satisfying than a couple of three-day-old muffins? Fifteen minutes of something super perks you up on a deeper level than two hours of something that is merely okay.

I found this out during my own struggle to stop baking "blackies." As my friends will tell you, I am famous for being able to flambé just about any food. (I scraped the burned bits off of my toast at breakfast just this morning.) I have a hand-carved sign in my kitchen that says, "If it ain't burnt Momma didn't cook it." While writing this book I have been running a consulting and coaching business, speaking around the country, and participating in a doctoral program. I know how to burn food . . . and my schedule.

"Happiance" came to me in a flash one morning as I was eating my overcooked eggs. What if you combined what made you happy with what nurtured you? Happy + Nurturance = Happiance. A double shot of playfulness plus pleasure. Sign yourself up! Boy, am I glad I did.

My Happiance break that day was buying colorful lingerie. As a child I was crazy for playing dress up. For some reason, if I feel sassy in my skivvies, I feel nurtured. It's like I have a great little (and I do mean little) secret. Maybe your Happiance is doing yoga or making candles. Go for what makes you smile.

Happy + Nurturance = Happiance

Then Happiance began working for my clients. One client, a healer here in California, had been thinking she *should* take a walk. But Shoulds almost never amount to a big bag of happy in my book, so we looked deeper. Walk schmalk. Her Happiance turned out to be something else. It was chewing bubble gum and going rollerblading that made her happy and filled her to the brim.

The Rest Test Game

Remember when your mom would remind you that it was bed time? If your sleep account is overdrawn, here's how to start making deposits again.

What you'll need: Yourself and your alarm clock.

1. *Bed Time.* Set your alarm clock . . . to remind you to go to bed! Set it 15 minutes earlier than your normal bed time for a week.
2. *Fab 15.* The following week, set your bed time alarm forward another 15 minutes. Keep moving it forward weekly until you are getting your full eight hours of Beauty Rest.
3. *Nap Time.* I am a big fan of cat naps. If you work out of your home, give them a try. If you spend your days in an office, see if you can find a quiet place to rest on a break. A 20-minute snooze can give you an incredible boost.
4. *Thank Yourself.* Thank yourself for making the choice to restore yourself.

So, what makes you happy and also nurtures your body and spirit? Singing at the top of your lungs? Playing with your pooch? Knitting? Check in with You-ville. If you are stumped for ideas, try taking a few minutes to do something you loved to do as a child.

The Happiance Game

Set aside at few minutes to replenish yourself. Don't you deserve 15 minutes of your day devoted entirely to you? Why not power down that PDA and cut yourself a little slice of happiness?

1. *Get Centered.* Take in three deep breaths of happy. Let out three deep breaths of blah. See. That was easy.

2. *Ask for the Greatest Good.* As Mayor, take a moment and claim your office, and ask that your self-nurturing choices are for the highest good of all.

3. *Set Your Intention.* Set the intention to nourish and honor yourself.

4. *Ask.* Ask yourself: How can I give myself some Happiance? What would give me a really big tickle today? What would make me feel replenished now? Give yourself a minute to notice what would fill you up right now.

5. *Surprise!* It's okay if it doesn't make sense. Happiness isn't logical. Do you want to buy yourself some flowers, get out your water colors and paint, put on your fuchsia undies? Whether it's frivolous or tender, let your "happy" surprise you.

6. *What's on the Kid's Menu?* If you're stymied, consider what you loved to do as a kid. If you were the neighborhood champ at making mud pies, maybe getting your hands in some clay is the ticket. If you loved

Barbie, Skipper, and Ken, then maybe a trip to the toy store would fill you up. Go for it.

7. *Write.* Write down what you want. That helps you to anchor it so it doesn't get lost in your busy day.

8. *Today If Possible.* Now, decide when you are going to give yourself this Happiance.Why delay your glee? Make plans to enjoy your Happiance today. Or at least sometime in the next seven days.

9. *Break It Down to Make It Happen.* Doing something small is enough to get your Happiance groove flowing. Let's say your Happiance is taking a walk along the seashore, but it's a long drive from wherever you are to the nearest beach. Ask yourself how you can give yourself some part of that experience today. Maybe it's soaking in a bath with sea salts added, or listening to vintage Hawaiian music, or admiring your sea shell collection after your evening walk around the block.

10. *Thank Yourself.* Thank yourself for making a positive choice to replenish yourself.

10

Pray to God...
and Talk to Your Girlfriends

A Woman's Biological Imperative

I'm here to tell you what you already know: We gals have a bigger need than the guys to connect and to yak. This too, like taking care of other people, is in our genes. If you're trying to get the man in your life to fulfill all of your interactional needs, you might be running into some snags. And there's a reason why. In lots of ways men and women speak different languages. That's why you need some Girlfriend Time. Think of it as your daily minimum female communication requirement.

Now don't be getting all huffy on me. I'm not saying that all humans aren't wonderful and wise. I'm not insinuating that men and women can't share deeply. No way, José. I'm not advocating withholding your thoughts and feelings from males. This isn't a dig at dudes. Men are different, not better or worse. Learning about a few of those contrasts can be a big help.

Size Does Matter

Stand by for the news flash: Men's and women's bodies are built differently (gee, thanks, Eli, for that groundbreaking discovery), and so are their brains. The corpus callosum in a woman's brain is larger. That's the passageway that connects the two sides of the brain. It allows women to bounce information back and forth in their brains faster than the fellas. It makes us the more verbal gender.

We talk more. You and I have more words we want to use up. A lot more. The larger channel means that we use oodles more words than the man next door does. And we have been doing it for a very long time. Even before the age of two, girls are twice as verbal as boys. That difference gets more pronounced as time goes on. Studies show that women use more than three times as many words as men. Richard Haier of the University of California, Irvine, reports that an average gal uses approximately 20,000 to 25,000 words a day. A typical guy will use 7,000 to 10,000 words in the same time span. Who better to use up some of those excess words with than a sista?

> *Leftover-Word Stew is best served to a gal pal.*

But wait, there's more. The larger corpus callosum means women's brains retrieve information quicker, so we can jump from one thing to the next. That also gives you the power to multitask. You can talk and do three other things at once. Men don't naturally make that leap. A guy once stopped me mid-conversation. "What were we talking about?" he asked. "You went so far from where we started, I forgot what we were talking about."

Men's brains typically retrieve one fact at a time. They talk like they are laying bricks. They focus on one fact brick, setting it in place and making sure it is well grounded in the cement of logic. They complete each step before moving on to the next fact. A + B + C + D leads to E. Women talk like they are making salad. We

> Guy Speak = laying bricks.
> Gal Speak = tossing salad.

multitask even when we talk. You and I tend to blithely fling in facts from three different piles without wasting time making sure they fit together. A + DD + G – H gets you to E.

Leave it to a thirteen-year-old to boil it all down. My young friend Taylor and I were taking a walk the other evening. I asked if he noticed any differences between the boys and girls in the sixth grade. "The guys are more straightforward. The girls are more complicated and they do weird things with clothes." When I asked why he thought there was a difference he said, "Back when we were cavemen, the dudes hunted the food. They had to concentrate and be quiet. The women were home making dinner and taking care of the kids, so they were talking all the time." Well, there you have it.

A Coffee Break Breakthrough

I used to feel a bit timid about raising the flag for Girlfriend Time. But as I was writing this chapter my friend Mimi told me about a recent study. Trust some amazing women scientists to back me up. The data they came up with is important, and the story is fantastic.

A couple of women researchers down the road at UCLA were

chatting one day in the break room. They were laughing at how in times of stress the women in the department came in to the coffee room, tidied up the lab, had coffee, and bonded. But when the men were under pressure, they holed up in their offices and were never seen.

The two women, Drs. Shelly Taylor and Laura Klein, had a mutual "aha" moment. Maybe the behavior of their fellow scientists was a clue for the species. What if women process stress differently than men? Wondering if they were onto something, they started digging. It didn't take too long to find out something very interesting. Ninety percent of all research data collected during the past 50 years of studying stress has been based on male test subjects. Hel-lo. That's hundreds of biological and behavioral studies and thousands of male subjects. What if that skewed the test results? Most of what we know about the famous fight-or-flight response is based on the responses of men. What if feminine folk respond to stress differently?

Oh, What a Difference a Y Chromosome Makes

Drs. Taylor and Klein began reviewing studies of females under stress. What started as a casual conversation lead to a revolutionary discovery. Females of many species—not just *Homo sapiens*—process stressors differently than the males. We have a secret additional weapon that the fellas don't have. They named it the "tend-and-befriend" response.

> *Want a stress buster? Tend and befriend, my friend.*

They discovered that when females are faced with a large

stressor, a small amount of the hormone oxytocin is released. Oxytocin is fondly called the love-and-cuddle hormone, and it has a calming effect. It's the powerful chemical that surges through the body when a woman breastfeeds her baby or has an intense emotional connection. That "feel-good juice" that a woman's body pumps out pushes her to look after her home and children and gather with other women during stressful times. It also buffers some of the modern-day ravages of an overstimulated fight-or-flight response, such as hypertension, aggressive behavior, and even the pull of substance abuse.

Once you actually go and do some tending and befriending, more oxytocin is released. Your hormones reward you by giving you more of what counters the stress and calms you down. Plus, the estrogen hormone seems to enhance oxytocin's effectiveness.

Men aren't so lucky. They produce high levels of testosterone when they're under stress. That helps them go out and kick some butt. However, it also short-circuits the calming effects of the smaller amount of oxytocin their body produces when it is under pressure.

Vitamin G

When my best friend, Barbara, said that maybe Girlfriend Time is a daily nutrient, a Vitamin G, I was literally bouncing off my chair. I thought that maybe Boo and I had had a UCLA moment—naming a new component in women that the men don't have. After my exultation, I Googled "Vitamin G" and my heart sank. Bummer. There already is a Vitamin G. It's another name for Vitamin B2.

As I read the research, however, I saw how much the two have in common. The need for Vitamin B2 increases during stressful situations. That's right. When times are tough, who are you going to call? Your girlfriends. Vitamin B2 aids in growth and general health. That fits too. Spending time with your girlfriends is good for your personal growth and creativity. Vitamin B2 promotes healthy skin, nails, and hair. Don't women spend a bit more time on healthy skin, nails, and hair than guys? Vitamin B2 helps metabolize carbohydrates, fats, and proteins. What woman doesn't want a better metabolism? Sure, the Vitamin G and Vitamin B2 connection isn't hard science, but hey, this is salad logic.

The More the Merrier... and the Healthier

Women's innate need for friendship may be one of the reasons they tend to outlive men. Study after study shows that having social ties is good for your health. Connecting with friends lowers your blood pressure, heart rate, and cholesterol. And as with Vitamin B2, you need the support of your loved ones

Balance your diet. Get a daily dose of Vitamin G!

and your community even more during challenging times.

More news on the Vitamin G front: Friends don't just help you live to a ripe old age, they help you live better. The Harvard Medical School's famed Nurses' Health Study found that the more friends a woman has, the less likely she is to get sick as she gets older. Isn't that great news? And the more friends, the more likely a woman is to feel she is leading a joyful life. Less aging and more joy . . . sign me up! The folks at Harvard discovered that not having close friends is as bad for your health as smoking.

If you're not in the habit of taking your Vitamin G girlfriend breaks, think again. Another Harvard study looked at how women handle what is considered the greatest stressor of all—the loss of their spouse. Most women who had close friends mourned the loss without becoming ill themselves. Those without friends were not always so fortunate—they were 60 percent more likely to become seriously ill.

Sometimes Conversation and Chocolate Are the Best Medicine

So, my friend, are *you* getting enough femme fab time? Probably not. Most women report that when they are busy, busy, busy, the time for friendships is the first thing to go. Americans today have one-third fewer close friends than 20 years ago, reported a recent study at Duke University. Sadly, the number of people who have no one to talk to has doubled to 25 percent. Girl time is pushed aside and forgotten as you spend

> *Your girlfriends see you through being broke, broken-hearted, and bad haircuts.*

more and more and more time at work. What is crazy is that you are giving up something that nurtures your mental and physical health.

Your girlfriends are a blessing. I know mine sure are. My best friend, Barbara, and I have seen each other through being broke, broken-hearted, and bad haircuts. Life just goes better with friendship. Even though she moved to Austin, Texas, four long years ago, we are still an integral part of each other's lives. Boo makes me laugh so hard I convulse, and her insight and kindness make me a better person.

Anyone would be lucky to have a friend like Annette. She puts so much love into everything she touches that she makes the world a better place. Once when I was sick she drove two hours to bring me soup. That meant soup, back-up soup, crackers, flowers, medicine, and water pitchers filled with apple and orange slices to make the water delicious. Now Andra, my fellow Kansan, keeps me honest. She is the one who will slap me upside the head and tell me I am being a bitch—or that the guy I am dating is . . . gay. I can't imagine how lackluster life would be without these friends. Spending time or even blabbing on the phone with any of them (well, not Andra—because calling her is like calling Uzbekistan; calls go in but none come out. You *visit* Andra, and when you need her, there is no better friend) makes whatever is going on better.

If you're in a hurry to get from funky to fabulous, grab a gal and do some gabbing. I'm not discounting the infinite wisdom each of us has inside. No one can ever know you better than you, my dear Mayor. However, if you are like the rest of us, you have blind spots in certain patches of You-ville. Your GPS may be tapping you gently on the shoulder. The Mental Board may be filibustering to get your attention. The Union of Emotions may be zooming up and down waving red flags. However, if you are staring right into a blind spot, it's hard to access your own knowing. Everybody is dumb about something. Friends can make out the details of a situation when you are so close it looks like a blur. To quote an old Dionne Warwick song, "That's what friends are for."

Jean's Story

Jean related an amazing story about the healing power of companionship. She had been ready to blow a gasket over a problem with her boyfriend. This otherwise wonderful guy was driving her batty talking about the woman who had dumped him a few months before they met. "Brenda, Brenda, Brenda. I was sick of hearing about Brenda," Jean told me. "I wanted romance, I wanted flowers, I wanted . . . courting! If he wasn't going to

> *Friends put you on the fast track to FAB.*

bring me flowers, at least he could send me a card. I can't tell you why I was so obsessed about him sending me a card . . . but that is how my crazy mind works."

Two girlfriends knocked on Jean's door to see if she wanted to go for a power hike just as she was about to pick up the phone and tell him off. They encouraged her to walk and whine. As she let her complaints flap in the wind she felt her whole body relax, and she began to see the issue a little more clearly. Barreling up and down the neighborhood hills moaning to her posse magically melted her boyfriend burden. She realized that she didn't need to nag about a silly little card.

One of her friends shared some GPS wisdom: "It seems like he shows affection in other ways. Maybe he isn't a card guy. It sounds like he gives you his undivided attention when you are with him. That sure sounds better than getting a card."

By the end of the walk, complaining about not getting a card or flowers was the last thing on Jean's mind.

If a good man isn't doing something, there is probably a good reason for it. That same night her boyfriend arrived at her door with both hands behind his back. He was carrying a card entitled "When You Meet an Angel"—"probably the most beautiful card ever written," Jean said to me. As Jean was telling him how much the card meant to her, he opened up and said that during one of their breakups, Brenda had literally thrown the cards he had sent her in his face. He shook his head. "I used to be romantic with flowers. But when I sent them they were never good enough, or she said I sent them just to get her to have sex with me. It took all the fun out of it." Ouch. Jean was thrilled that she had talked with her girlfriends rather than lousing up a great thing.

Vitamin G Fab Time

Connecting and sharing with a friend is manna from the heavens to us women. If you are being challenged by a day when everything is going frizzy and fly-away (a Bad Hair Day?), call a girlfriend. If you have words to use up at the end of the day, call one of your gals.

What you will need: 30 minutes of private time with a girlfriend. A timer is helpful.

1. *Invite.* Ask a girlfriend if you can schedule some Vitamin G Fab Time. If you can't meet in person, meet on the phone. Arranging the time ahead of time sets up a powerful intent for an out-of-the-ordinary get-together.
2. *An Interruption-Free Zone.* Turn off your cell phone. Take any other steps you need to so you won't be disturbed. The world will survive if you take a half hour for you and your friend. Give each other the gift of your undivided attention.
3. *Center, Ask for the Greatest Good, and Set Your Intention.* Make this time special and sacred. Start your Vitamin G Fab Time by centering yourselves and focusing on your breathing. Ask that only the highest good for all concerned comes forth during your session and as a result of your session. Set an intention for deep listening and deep sharing.

4. *10 + 5 = Fab Time.* Let each of you share for 10 minutes. Followed by 5 minutes of supportive feedback from the one who has been listening. Crazy as it sounds, setting a timer for 10 minutes and 5 minutes is very helpful.

5. *Let the Speaker Speak.* Let the speaker say what she has to say without a single interruption. We gals tend to jump into each other's sentences. Uninterrupted talk time may be a new and profoundly healing experience.

6. *Listen with Your Heart.* When you are in the Vitamin G listener's seat, set your intention to listen deeply. Remember, no interruptions. Your job is to give your pal the gift of your undivided attention. Listening deeply may be something surprisingly new.

7. *Feedback Time Is the Speaker's Time.* During the 5 minutes of feedback, it's the one who just shared who directs what's happening. She can ask for words of support or encouragement, or for a hug, or even 5 minutes of silence if that's what she needs.

8. *What I Like about You.* When both of you have had a turn, close the Vitamin G session by naming three qualities you appreciate in each other.

9. *Thank Yourself.* Thank yourself and your pal for making the positive choice to give and receive support with full attention.

11

The Low-Criticism Diet

Love the One You're With

Do you look at yourself in the mirror and see your lumps and bumps rather than your beauty? Do you have more diet books than cookbooks? Do you feel guilty after eating certain foods . . . and then eat more of them because your relationship to food seems hopeless? Boy, have I had to learn this one the hard way—maybe you have too. I was a closet eater throughout my teens (if no one sees me eating, the calories won't stick). As soon as I got my first set of car keys I graduated to being a drive-by eater (hey, if I am moving, the calories won't stick).

The Tale of the Evil Twin Zippers

In second grade, I went from petite to porky. The horror of that fact didn't hit me until the morning of Field Day. That was the day the whole elementary school got together to play games outside like tug of war, the three-legged race, and gunny-sack jumping. We even got to wear shorts to school.

Right before the first event began, I ran inside to go to the bathroom. But the twin zippers of my shorts, pulled tight over my bulging belly, wouldn't budge. Agh. I was wearing the two-zipper shorts I was so proud of. Not one zipper but two—how cool. I started panting. I r-e-e-e-eally had to go. Pulling, tugging. The more I panicked, the less the zippers moved. Finally, a warm flow ran down my inner thigh. I stood in shock as the flood of pee *ran* across the floor and out the door of the school's teensy one-stall bathroom.

"I guess I am going to have to fix that sink after all." The school janitor was walking by the door at that very moment and saw the trickle coming out the door. I was already red with shame at having peed in my pants. Now someone else knew about it. And Mr. Sprooty was a big talker—within the next 35 minutes the whole school would know. My excess weight had turned my beloved twin-zipper shorts from fashion statement to torture chamber—and turned me into an object of humiliation. That was the moment I declared war on my own body.

The Fat Trap

Unfortunately, more and more girls are falling into the trap of viewing their body as the enemy. Just recently I took the beautiful—and slender—11-year-old daughter of my best friend to dinner. I was shocked when, as we

No one wins the shame game.

left the restaurant, she saw her reflection in a window and pulled at her hips complaining, "Ugh, I can't stand my love handles." Researcher J. J. Brumberg has found that 53 percent of all American girls aged 13 are dissatisfied with their bodies whether they are actually overweight or not. That figure jumps to 73 percent for 17-year-olds. And an ongoing study funded by the National Heart, Lung, and Blood Institute reported that 40 percent of the 9- and 10-year-olds surveyed had already tried to lose weight at some point in their young lives.

The Quiet Diet

I was one of those girls. I started dieting in third grade. Who could blame me? Linda Covell, Pam Miller, and Debbie Earsman used to meet in a circle on the playground. When I wanted to join they told me, "The only people in our club are under 75 pounds." I remember shaking my leg every moment of every class in third grade in hopes of exercising off my second-grade girth. I learned, even as a 9-year-old, to judge my value by the numbers on the scale. The school nurse shook her head when she saw I had grown several inches and not gained any weight for the entire school year. I, however, was elated.

I continued my quiet diet (I was far too ashamed to tell anyone), and by sixth grade I looked like everyone else on the outside. But my image of myself was Fat Girl. Camouflaging my

Are you obsessing over the size of your gut or butt?

thighs was the main consideration with every single outfit I wore through my teens. Embarrassing high school admission #1: I wore a girdle under my pants because I thought I was so fat. Embarrassing high school admission #2: I used to feign illness in order to avoid pool parties or other activities that required wearing shorts or a bathing suit. Embarrassing high school admission #3: My nickname on the field hockey team was Motor Butt. If I could have taken a machete to my hips, I would have done so gladly.

The Perfect Diet . . . for a Gerbil

Even though I was always dieting, I never believed I was eating lean enough. Lettuce, celery, and apples were the only foods I ate without a pang of guilt. Since I could never stay very long on that diet, custom-designed for a gerbil, I binged in frustration. In college, my car was littered with telltale wrappers from the Twinkies and Milky Ways I ate when no one was watching. A day was judged good or bad according to how I managed my war with food. Had I prevailed and eaten just fruit and salad? Or had I been ambushed by the enemy, chocolate? Yet I never felt thin enough. Even when I finally achieved my elusive ideal weight of 110 pounds, I still saw my fat instead of my leanness.

> *Do you rate your day by how well you wage your war with food?*

Those women in the magazines could be thin, happy, and have it all. Why didn't my workouts at the gym and living on varieties of lettuce give me the same result?

Comparison Is a Game You Can Never Win

"I wish I looked like Cindy Crawford," said Cindy Crawford in a recent interview. Wha-a-a-t? How could that gorgeous supermodel want to look like . . . herself? Because it takes a small battalion of makeup artists, hair stylists, trainers, and wardrobe and lighting experts, plus of course airbrushing, to make Cindy Crawford look like Cindy Crawford. Can you believe that even Cindy has Bad Hair Days? Even Cindy sucks in her gut?

Have you caught yourself playing the checkout-line size-up game—rating other women's "having it together" factor by the size of their hips and thighs, and then measuring yourself against them? I hope not. It's excruciating.

If you are judging your insides by somebody else's outside, you are always going to lose. Besides, that person whose exterior you are admiring could be completely miserable walking about in their You-ville, and you wouldn't know it. Comparing yourself is founded on the judgment that you're not good enough as you are. It cuts you off from the Great Good, who sees the divine essence in you and everyone else, who knows you as far more beautiful than words can describe even when you can't zip up your fat pants.

What Are You Really Hungry For?

I used to think I would only be lovable if my thighs didn't touch. That's pretty bonkers. Where is it written that thin people deserve more love? In fact, sensuality and sexiness are entirely an inside job. It's that confidence that's so compelling. But in that crazy 20-something head of mine, a good person was one who eats salads and has measurements like 36-24-36. I wasn't perfect, and my thighs were the proof. The Universe is kind enough to substantiate your unconscious beliefs. I was married to a man who graciously validated my insane theory. He constantly told me I was too fat—and I was a size 8 at the time.

What a big old bunch of hooey! Don't fool yourself the way I did. Those crazy chocolate cravings aren't about filling up with food. Your stomach pangs are driven by your heart pangs. I yearned for kindness and comfort, and eating chocolate and mounds of cinnamon toast was the only way I knew to find it. Yet no amount of food could satisfy my appetite.

Yes, that hunger you feel may actually be for more TLC (Tender Loving Care). And even though this goes against just about everything the culture tells you, you're the best person to give yourself the love you are craving. You are the Mayor of your wonderful town, and no one is better equipped to fill you up just the way you want.

A Message from the Fatty Wear Council

The person who first introduced me to the concept of loving and accepting my body just as it is might as well have been speaking Sudanese. Or Martian, for that matter. I thought: "This guy is a crackpot. If I accept myself as I am, all hell will break out. If I stop beating myself up over eating half a cookie, I'll be eating three dozen cookies for every meal. Before I know it, I'll be 600 pounds and they'll have to cut me out of my double-wide trailer." Ha! I wasn't going to fall for that "accept yourself as you are" propaganda. When it came to the serious issue of weight, I knew there was a conspiracy. He was probably an agent hired by the Fatty Wear Council.

My friend was undaunted. "Acceptance is the first law of the

Universe." I didn't have a clue about what he meant. He carefully explained that approving of myself whatever my size would take away the very self-judgment that fueled my overeating. It sounded nutty, but he had piqued my interest.

Not long afterwards, I met a woman who seemed to glow with health. And she had thin thighs, so I paid particular attention to what she had to say. "When I decided to stop beating myself up and start accepting the way I look in the mirror, things changed. It took away a lot of my need to binge. Giving myself permission to eat chocolate now and then meant that I didn't crave it as much."

Hmm. This self-love stuff was beginning to make sense. Food, she was saying, did not have to be the enemy, and my body did not have to be a battleground. If I didn't beat myself up, my binges wouldn't have so much ammo to fire at me.

The Cycle of Overeating

Self-nagging is one of the most fattening things on the planet. It's what drives the cycle of overeating. Debra Waterhouse reports that according to a Stanford University study, weight loss doesn't necessarily improve body image. Rather, the reverse is true: body acceptance—a low-criticism diet—is the best weight-loss program. The women who were the most at peace with their body were twice as likely to lose weight than those who were wildly dissatisfied with the way they looked. That's why beating yourself up after eating some chocolate cake often leads to eating the entire cake.

Here's how this works:

Step One: *The Impossible Dream Syndrome. Glancing through the most recent copy of your favorite magazine, you take a good look at Madonna's arms. You think your arms should look like that, forgetting about the army of workout trainers, Pilates teachers, and yoga instructors she has to help with those triceps. Those Shoulds are a slippery bunch. Before you've had time to mull it over, they've got you comparing yourself to a picture in a magazine and coming out on the losing end. Then you assign yourself a Completely Impossible Task: "I will look like Madonna if it kills me. From now on I will never eat dessert."*

This leads to Step Two: The Wrong, Wrong, Wrong Syndrome. When you decree an unrealistic expectation for yourself, you are setting yourself up to fail. If you are a human being, at some point you will probably eat a piece of cake. Sure enough, at some point you yield to that slice of orange pecan torte with lemon frosting smiling at you from the dessert tray.

Breaking your promise to yourself sends you right into Step Three: The Scolding Syndrome: "You are such a fat slob. You ate cake again. What a disgusting loser."

To lessen the pain of flogging yourself emotionally, you go into Step Four: The Oh, Screw It Syndrome. "Why bother. I blew my diet already. I think I will eat the entire tray of desserts." Afterward, when you see the wreckage of the tray strewn with crumbs, you get so disgusted that you declare you will never touch a morsel of dessert again; you're going for Madonna arms—and the cycle begins all over again.

Band-Aid on a Plate

Food can be a great regulator of feelings. That's why we often turn to comfort foods when we're upset. If feeling angry or sad wasn't particularly popular in the house you grew up in, a second serving of potatoes may be your response of choice even today. It seems easier than acknowledging the pain that is present. When your stomach is busy digesting, it doesn't feel the rawness of emotions.

Oddly enough, we sometimes eat to avoid experiencing deep pleasure or joy, as well. One client went on a candy bar binge the day after she got the biggest contract of her career. Another client started eating loads of desserts and doubling her drinking when she met her future husband. Gay and Katie Hendricks call this the Upper Limits Phenomenon. It sure seems crazy, but we have a thermostat for happiness and success, and we can be as uncomfortable on the high end of the happiness scale as we are on the low end.

Sweetness beyond the Sugar

Even when you're absorbed in doing something you love, if it means you're ignoring the small ways you need to show yourself love daily, the other parts of You-ville will try to fill the lack by going for the sugar. Though

> *You are the sweetness you crave.*

friends had told Cathy it was a completely impractical choice, Cathy had followed her heart and was studying to become a minister. She added her theological studies to her long hours at a corporate job. She adored her studies, yet she found that she was eating chocolate by the pound. I asked Cathy, "Are you being sweet enough with yourself?"

In the mad dash to fulfill her dream she had ignored giving herself the very kindness and compassion she wanted to one day share with a congregation. Craving something sugary was a sign that she needed to give herself the sweetness of her own attention. Figuring out what to do didn't take a huge amount of time. One way was to take short breaks during the day. She called these her "Sugar Time." To her amazement, as soon as she began giving herself the confectionary comfort of her own caring, she didn't need so much external sugar.

A Diet You Can Live With

Leading nutritionists are concluding that cultivating a grateful attitude toward your body actually helps you assimilate your food better and have fewer cravings. Elaine Finesilver, a top nutritionist in Aspen, Colorado, and Beverly Hills, California, asks her clients to spend time each day thanking their bodies and appreciating them for the wonderful job they are doing.

Am I saying that loving acceptance, and its cousin, gentleness, can actually enhance your health? You bet. Believe it or not, deciding to love your body just as it is, right now, lumps, bumps, and all, is a crucial step in breaking the cycle of combat with your weight. Take it from one who knows.

If you have had a pattern of overfeeding or underappreciating that glorious body you are living in, The Low-Criticism Diet (the TLC Diet) may be just the one for you. It's tough to eat too many green leafy vegetables. It's just as hard to give yourself too much kindness. What if you cut down on the Krispy Kremes of comparing yourself to someone else's body shape? What if you went through the internal cupboards in your mind and got rid of all the junk-food berating of yourself? The TLC Diet could be the last weight release program you'll ever need.

Here's the diet plan:

Step One: *Get Real. Stop scanning the horizon for the newest fad diet. Stop comparing yourself to every female form the media presents to you. As Mayor of You-ville, your very first responsibility is the health and well-being of your town. Pass a law banning the thought of going from a size 14 to a size 4 for at least a week. Give yourself a breather and let who you are be peachy-keen. Okay, you don't look like a super model. Accept yourself as you are and watch your mood lift. Once you stop the war with your body, you are more open to listening to its innate wisdom.*

And get real about what you can actually do—which means, take it in manageable steps. What small action can you take toward a healthier you? Maybe today you will have one less donut and spend 15 minutes walking. Maybe you will drink a Big Gulp of water instead of Coke. Try turning off the TV while you are eating dinner—paying attention to what you eat while you eat it is a big plus in feeling satiated. Writing down what you eat is another way to get real about what's going into your mouth. Another powerful strategy is to eat only while you are sitting. And if you want to be very savvy, only eat while you are eating. When you get conscious about what you are actually eating, it fills you up faster and you don't need to eat as much.

Step Two: Get Full, Full, Full. Setting up an unattainable goal (say, losing 67 pounds before your annual convention next month) based on what you can't have (say, never eating sugar ever, ever, ever again) is a recipe for feeling famished. As you've heard me say before, what you focus on grows. When you focus on not eating any sweets, what do you crave? Cookies, cake, and cherry cobbler.

On the TLC Diet you zero in on what fills you up. Pay attention to what you do well and celebrate it. Prize yourself and your body unconditionally. Focus on the good in others as well—it's the best dessert! Appreciation is one of the most satisfying things on the planet.

Step Three: Get Gentle. In the overeating cycle you scolded yourself for your slips and falls. On The Low-Criticism Plan you find ways of cherishing and being patient with yourself. It's easy to get frustrated when you are changing a habit. It takes a bit of work at the beginning. Be gentle with yourself anyway. Start listening to your internal dialogue. If you are like me and have given yourself years of abusive self-talk, cut those voices off at the pass. Override them with statements like "I am patient and gentle with myself as I grow and learn," "I love you just as you are," "I love me no matter what I think or say or do." That's how affirmations work. There's never a bad time to serve up some TLC for yourself or someone else.

Step Four: *Get Grateful. The old model ended up with hopelessness and defeat. Instead, name your victories. Find three things to celebrate about yourself right this moment. Even if it's as simple as the fact that you brushed your hair this morning. Be grateful that you have hair and let that appreciation spread through your whole body. Take a few minutes to infuse your body with thankfulness—in the shower is a great place to do this. There is no downside to being grateful.*

Lowering Your Criticism Lowers Your Weight

That's the diet. Cut down on your self-criticism—don't even try to cut out being critical altogether. That's another Impossible Dream. Just aim to cut it in half. Substitute more self-appreciation. As you begin to track critical self-talk you may be shocked by how negative you have been with yourself—and also delighted with how good you feel as you start to prize yourself. Take action steps: Sit down when you eat and put your attention on what you

> *Lower your self-badgering and watch your bingeing back off.*

are chewing. Take a moment to give thanks for the nourishing food before you. Give yourself daily servings of the loving that food symbolizes by thanking your body. Cut back on carping. That way you are giving yourself the caring and acceptance that you really, actually, deeply desire.

It works. I shared The Low-Criticism Diet with a coaching client. She released ten pounds she hadn't been able to lose in three years of dieting and workouts. Her officemates, her husband, and even the nurse at her doctor's office were amazed at how she lost weight simply and quickly.

How do you decipher what is and what isn't self-criticism? One trick is to keep in mind the question "Would I talk to a baby this way?"

Your Alliance of Body Parts is a great friend whatever its shape and size. Besides, it's the only body you've got, so why not love the one you're with? If all this lovey-dovey business with yourself is new, take it in small steps. And cut yourself some slack when you want a piece of pie. Diet expert Dr. Paul Rivas suggests an 80/20 guideline. If you eat wisely 80 percent of the time and give yourself freedom 20 percent of the time, you are likely to be very healthy. Have the pie. Enjoy it. Savor it. And add a healthy dollop of loving self-acceptance.

Give Yourself Some TLC

Most women look in the mirror and criticize something. Now that you are the Mayor, you can choose to change that. You can go into a rundown neighborhood in You-ville and turn things around. Yep, it's time to love your least favorite body part.

Next time you're standing in front of the mirror, go ahead and look yourself in the eyes and declare, "I love you just the way you are," or "I love you, I honestly love you." Or hum the lines from another schmaltzy '70s love song. If you aren't going to love yourself, you can't expect somebody else to do the job for you. Besides, the truth is that you really are beautiful inside and out.

What you'll need: A few extra minutes during your morning routine and your body moisturizer.

1. *Center Yourself.* Take three deep breaths. On the inhales, breathe in love for yourself just the way you are. On the exhales, let out fault-finding. Ahh!
2. *Ask for the Greatest Good.* As Mayor, take a moment and claim your office, and ask for acceptance of yourself for the highest good.
3. *Set Your Intention.* Set an intention to befriend your bod.
4. *Pick a Part.* While you lather up in the shower, notice any part of You-ville that's been beaten down for a long

time. Give it some loving attention. The body part you like the least is the one that needs the most love.

5. *Or Your Whole Birthday Suit.* If you say you hate your entire body, then lavish your loving over your whole physique, every part.

6. *Talk to Yourself.* Tell your body or body part that you appreciate all it does for you. Hey, you're in the shower, who's going to hear you?

7. *Thank Your Curves.* After the shower when you're putting on body lotion, love each lump and bump. Feel the warmth of your heart fill your hands as you apply loving to any part of you that you've called ugly.

8. *Why Stop?* Take today and cherish this part of your body or your entire body. All day. Notice if your criticism output lessens while you're at it.

9. *Mirror, Mirror.* Whenever you spot yourself in a mirror through the day, note your most positive features (we all have them) and pay yourself a compliment.

10. *More TLC.* Get creative and have fun finding ways to lower your criticism and raise your TLC.

11. *Thank Yourself.* Thank yourself for making the fabulous choice to love all of you.

12

Defrost TV Dinner Reality

Why Settle for Shoulds?
You Deserve a Life You Savor

D o you feel like you're in a rut? If you could take a bite out of your day, would it taste bland? If you're wondering who stole the zesty zip out of your life, the likely culprits are what I call the Shoulds—your expectations and unconscious assumptions. Shoulds zap the nutrients right out of the present moment. They whisk the freshly prepared gourmet dinner version of your existence off the table and serve you the TV dinner version instead. Why waste your life's calories on Shoulds when you could spend them on something fabulous?

Our society floods us with fixed menus for happiness. Every day you see images of people going from crappy to happy because they switched deodorants. Every day you see a family going

> *You can never get enough of what you don't really want.*

from glum to gleeful because they got a deep dish pizza. These images are designed to create a Should inside you. You should do . . . be . . . have . . . more. Even if they don't inspire you to run out and buy a wagon-wheel-sized slab of dough and cheese, you still unconsciously buy into the American Dream: stuff equals happiness.

I beg to differ. You can never get enough of what you don't really want.

Sure, it's easy to roll your cart down the grocery aisle of life and toss in prepackaged ambitions. Big house. Big car. Not so big butt. It's easy to reach into the frozen food case and grab cultural standards. "Everyone wants this stuff, it must be good," you mumble as you pop those icy boxes of prefab expectations into the freezer of your mind. Sure, you know what frozen chicken pot pie will taste like—every time. Its doughy crust and soggy carrots are comforting and familiar. And boring. You deserve better.

If waking up in a McMansion with a Jacuzzi and a master suite has the appeal of day-old scrambled eggs for you, so be it. It's your choice. You could own a big house, or not. Maybe your dream has you living in a rain forest helping the indigenous people to preserve their land. Don't disregard the vibrant, quirky freshness of You-ville. Faux is never fab. The culture offers you ready-made objectives, but a success determined by somebody else never tastes as sweet as one that is genuine for you.

Faux is never fab.

Jan's Story

Shoulds can even affect your health. Jan was single and in her late thirties, and at the top of her Should List sat the Big

Should: Get Married. It was such a touchy topic that no family member was allowed to bring it up. Meanwhile, finding a husband turned into a mission Jan managed like an MBA research project. She kept a detailed notebook of all her internet dating candidates. She even color coded them into different categories. When Jan read Carl's profile, she found it included everything on her list. He was successful and spiritual (even though he wasn't particularly attractive). Much to her surprise, he was also open to having kids. She gave him bonus points because he made her laugh. Each item on her Marry This Man List was checked off, so they got engaged.

Yet as the wedding date grew closer Jan had to face the obvious: the lack of passion between them. Where was the chemistry? (She had forgotten to include sexual sizzle on her list.) She tried to hypnotize herself by running through his positive qualities inventory over and over in her head. Maybe her affections would grow. They didn't. Maybe if they went to therapy they'd get closer. They didn't.

Jan was getting sick frequently. She felt so bad that she went to a holistic doctor, who said her adrenal system was pretty much shot. In fact, Jan was so exhausted that the adrenal supplements she was taking, which would have been enough to pep up a small army, did her very little good. Jan wasn't listening to Jan-ville, so her town was shutting down the energy supply in order to get her attention.

One day the doctor surprised her with a question: "Are you in a relationship that isn't working?" He let her know that her vitality might not come back until she was doing what pleased her instead of what she thought she should do.

It took a few weeks, but Jan got up the courage to break off her engagement with Carl. To her astonishment, within two weeks of the breakup, her body was so full of energy that the doctor took her off the supplements altogether. She still isn't married, but she is content and healthy. Last I heard, she was off to savor a Girlfriend Getaway at a local spa.

The Should-O-Meter

When you hear a Should happening in your head, does it make you feel funkier or more fabulous? Thought so. Consider putting a big neon sign over the word "should." Imagine bull horns going off every time "should" comes out of your mouth. That's the Should-O-Meter—a warning system that announces: "The Mayor has left the building." As the Big Cheese, you're the one who is qualified to decide your internal standards. But "should" answers to the demands of society (whoever the heck that is) and the internal Criticism Committee, not the Mayor.

Shoulds seem to arise when you are doing something out of obligation rather than inspiration (like going to your high school reunion). Or when you are nervous or not ready to make a step that you are pushing yourself to take (like going to your high school reunion). Or when some- one is pressuring you to conform to an artificial standard when you don't really want to (like your mom pressuring you to go to your high school reunion).

Is your Should-O-Meter telling you: "The Mayor has left the building"?

Shoulds are not the same as Have Tos. Paying your taxes,

for instance, is not a Should. It's nonnegotiable; it's a fact of life. You need to eat, sleep, and pay your taxes—unless you are willing to spend the rest of your life hiding from the IRS. But do you really want to trot off to the deepest, darkest woods of Montana and never sip another Decaf Mochaccino? Ever again? There are hefty consequences if you don't follow through with a fact of life. Shoulds don't carry the same hefty price tag—you just think they do.

If it's negotiable, then you have a choice. It's your life. Why not choose to make it a fabulous one?

What's in the Deep Freeze?

So how do you turn down the Should-O-Meter and shut me up? One way is to look at your unexamined Shoulds. Are there things you have settled for without actually choosing them? Perhaps your job is something your family and friends expected you to do. Perhaps you love zesty bright colors but your closet is full of multiple shades of beige so you'll fit in. Perhaps you live in the town where you grew up simply because none of your friends have moved. Why not poke around in your mental ice box and see what kinds of assumptions are in there? Prepackaged notions about money and relationship are stock items for most folks.

Here are a few of the unconscious beliefs I discovered at the back of my own internal frig: You should be married (or at least have a boyfriend). You should be nice (or at least look like you're nice). You should not get angry (or at least don't let people see you lose it). You should be thinner

Why not defrost your decisions?

than you are (or at least be on a diet). You should have more money saved (or at least have a lot of good stuff to show for spending your money).

So what's in your deep freeze? Opening up the freezer door to take a look is the first step in finding out. The warm incoming air—your attention—disrupts the frozen environment and starts the thaw. Simple awareness is enough to start defrosting the frozen mess that's been tucked away in your unconscious.

You know what it's like to find icy bags of frozen foodstuffs plastered to the back corners of your Frigidaire. It's as though the frost takes over and everything gets stuck together. It's the same in your mind. Prying assumptions apart is harder if you haven't examined what's in there for a while. Be patient. Ice is just water that hasn't melted yet.

Pull out one internal expectation at a time and take a good look. Ask yourself, "Does this work for me?" Is it a concept that makes you feel more expansive and inspired, or is it old and freezer-burned, its flavor gone? Just like that old bag of frozen peas, you can keep it or let it go.

> *Let go of the prefab and the drab.*

Once you have become aware of a prefab expectation that doesn't line up with what's juicy for you, send it on its way. But how? Take a small step. Any move toward the positive will do. A pint-sized change (going for a walk, changing your shoes, signing up for a weekly drawing class) has a big impact. Why? Instead of following the dictates of an unexamined expectation, you are consciously doing something empowering. As you make more self-honoring choices the momentum builds. The new becomes part of your behavior. That's how a seemingly insignificant choice can eventually have huge impact on larger-scale things, like your quality of life.

Ashley was the harried young mother of two rugged boys, ages two and four. "A good mom doesn't leave her kids. Besides, taking time for yourself is selfish" was one of her Shoulds. But losing her temper for the umpteenth time, she had to admit that she needed a break. Ashley dragged herself to a salsa class at the Y. She felt guilty leaving her boys, and she didn't like the class. . . .

Nope, guess again. She loved the class! Not only that, she had more energy the next day, and more patience. Playing salsa music helped her get the dusting done. She let herself get more sultry in the bedroom. She found herself getting more creative and having more fun with her kids. Eighteen months later, she was teaching a beginner's salsa class at the very same Y. If you ask Ashley's sons, they will tell you she is now a better mom. One small syncopated step changed her life.

Change a Letter, Change Your Attitude

Want a fast way to defrost your unexamined assumptions and beliefs? Change "should" to "could." That simple switch of letters gives you back your power to pick out your fab. "Should" quietly implies that you are a loser—if you had your act together, you would have already checked the Shoulds off your To Do list. "Could" suggests that you can do it if you want to but you know you don't have to. And you are super yummy either way. You are the one who decides. And being a woman, you get to change your mind about it sixteen times before lunch.

It makes me sit up a little taller to know I can give some of my hefty Shoulds a letter transplant. Hey, I could be married—or not! Yippee, I could be thinner—or not! Hot dog, I could have more money saved—or not! Try it on some of the Shoulds stashed in your freezer. It sure feels good.

Pass the Pleasers, Please

Another way to reawaken yourself is to give yourself whatever deeply, profoundly pleases you—a Pleaser. Is it drive-across-town good? That's a Pleaser. It doesn't need to make sense to anyone but you and the people of You-ville. Why not take a chomp out of the delicious dish of what deeply delights you? Remember Meg Ryan pounding the table in *When Harry Met Sally?* Yea, baby, serve yourself your own version of whatever she was having, and watch your life become juicier.

What are your Pound the Table Pleasers?

Speaking of drive-across-town good, it's been eye-opening to spend some time in a place where they take their Pleasers seriously: Italy. (My sister and her family live there.) The Italians have so much to teach the rest of us about the *dolce vita* of Pleasers. A Roman thinks nothing of driving two hours to have a cup of coffee in Naples. Ask ten residents of the Eternal City and you'll find they all agree. Sure, the Romans sneer at the Neapolitans. They make jokes about Naples all the time. But they know the coffee in Naples is the best in the world (it's something to do with the water—go figure), and a really good cup of coffee is worth the drive.

What's Your Dolce Vita?

If you can't make it to Naples for a cup of coffee, you can still please-ify your day. You may not know what you want to do with your life, but you do know what you'd really like to wear today or have for lunch. A Pleaser isn't a craving on steroids. It's that small pleasure that has the power to brighten an entire morning, sometimes an entire day. It isn't something you'll regret later. It's often sensory, though it doesn't have to be. Pleasers live in the present moment, so they change often. That cup of cocoa with whipped cream that made your eyelids flutter yesterday may not be what you relish today. You need to pay attention to what would tickle You-ville in the moment.

Let's go back to the Italians. How do they make their weekend plans? Consult the internet? No way. Look at the current events section of the newspaper? Absolutely not. On a Saturday morning an Italian will stick his or her head out the window to see which way the wind is blowing. Will it be a luscious, sunny day at the beach or a better day for a stroll in the mountains? The direction of the wind will tell you. The Italians go for the best cup of coffee and the best day at the beach possible.

Your Pleaser Meter

It may not sound like a big deal, but taking a walk in my neighborhood rates very high on my own Pleaser roster. I've lived in some scummy places. During the struggling actress days, I lived in Harlem in a building with a sign above the front door that said "No repairing on cars." There were drug dealers on the corner and a bodega that sold Betty Jane Donut Gems and co-caine across the street. Now I live on a tree-lined street one block from a golf course. There is no one more grateful to live in my zip code. If I could kiss every rose, lily, and magnolia I see on my morning stroll, I would.

If you are a woman who works long hours and likes a bit of retail therapy, the Shopportunity Game may be just the ticket for you. Every month you earmark fifty dollars purely for Pleasers. Clients have bought boas, wands, a kooky dog lamp, a tiara collection, and the largest $12.99 stuffed bunny on the face of the earth. One common trait among shopportunity trea-sures is that they are saturated with color. I don't know of a client who has ever come back with something beige, brown, or black.

Drab Isn't Fab

Color is powerful. The next time you are out driving, notice how many fast food restaurants have the color red in their logo. Why red? It's been proven as the color that stimulates hunger. Huge amounts of research and money go into determining the precise hue used in the packaging of most products.

Why does the business world give such great attention to color? Because it works. Color communicates on so many levels without the burden of words and is one of our fastest signaling sys-tems. For example, a black fly buzzing around your kitchen is merely an annoyance. Put yellow and black stripes on the same

Take the color elevator to a better mood.

basic shape and your response is very different. Green on the grass is great. Green growing on your hamburger bun is gross.

You are probably drawn to certain colors. Why not choose the hues that make you feel luscious and wear them? Pleaser Wear is a surefire way to add some pep to the start of your day. Think of it as "better living through fashion." When you get dressed in the morning, put on at least one thing that makes you smile—happy shoes, snappy bra, goofy socks, whatever makes you gleeful. Sometimes finding your inner beauty starts on the outside.

Happy Shoes, Happy Girl

As you know, I am a confessed shoe freak. When I travel, I often slip in some shoe shopping as a Pleaser break. Oh, baby, when I saw the lavender suede Bond girl go-go boots, they said Pleaser all over them. Sure, I should have bought the same style in brown . . . but why bother? Every time I put on my lavender love boots, I walk with extra sass in my step. When I attended a meeting with the bigwigs at a media company, everything about my ensemble was tasteful. Caramel blazer, cream pants, a vintage pin. I couldn't help myself. I just had to wear my loud lavender Pound the Table Pleaser Boots.

Sure, it was a Fashion Don't. But it was a Happy Do. I met almost twenty people, from the head of development to the production assistants. Without fail, every person said, "Wow. What cool boots." That, my dear, is the power of a Pleaser.

So what are your Pound the Table Pleasers? Have at least one a day, and call me in the morning if you aren't feeling better.

Cassie's Story

Cassie was a numbers girl. She measured her business success by the stats of her e-zine and product sales, and making her numbers meant working insane hours. Having a weekend, a vacation, or a hobby was as foreign to her as saying hello in Farsi. Yet her bank account wasn't growing rapidly, and she was on the edge of burnout.

I suggested that she get started on the 2x2x4 Coaching Program (twice the money with half the work and four times the fun). She scoffed at the idea of making more money while working less. But she was desperate, so she gave it a try. When I asked her to think of something she loved doing (the four times the fun part), as with most folks, the word almost jumped out of her mouth. For Cassie, it was "quilting!"

When Cassie began working at home, she'd dutifully tucked the persimmon silk piece she had been stitching underneath her bed, where it languished for six years as her business overtook her house and her life. Cassie expected to work hard on her work until she turned 65, and resume stitching when she retired.

My Should-O-Meter went off. What unexamined Should was freezing up Cassie's fun muscle? A foray into the freezer uncovered the belief that she *should* work hard to get ahead. She doubted that quilting would help her 2x2x4 Plan, but she pulled out the beautiful quilt anyway and got out her needle and thread. After a few days she was jazzed. She stopped work every day at 7:00 PM so she could pick up her sewing. Within a month she decided to enter a quilt in the state fair.

Giving herself time for fun led to other breakthroughs. She

realized it was insane to spend her $200-an-hour talents packing boxes, so she hired a fulfillment house. Seemingly out of the blue, significantly larger contracts began appearing—she was on the way to doubling her income. Now curious about other ways to make more money with less work, Cassie discovered the miracles of online affiliate programs, which pay referral fees for recommending their services. She had been referring people anyway so this was no extra work, and the income was substantial. It was the easiest money of her life, she said.

Last week she sent me an email saying she had just gotten a $7,000 affiliate program check. Her income was twice what it had been six months earlier for the second consecutive month. Doing a little something that pleased her had fueled the transformation. Substituting the 2x2x4 Plan for the belief that she *should* fill each moment with work opened her up to fresh ways of thinking and new avenues of income and support. It can happen for you too.

Change a Letter, Change Your Day

This is so simple.

1. When you catch yourself either saying or thinking "should" ("I should eat less junk food"),
2. Replace it with "could" ("I could eat less junk food— or not"). Remember, you are the Mayor of You-ville. You call the shots! Let it sink in.
3. Thank yourself for giving yourself the freedom to be fine just as you are.

Pick a Pleaser Game

Strange as it seems, clients often have a harder time giving themselves Pleasers than adding more projects to their To Do pile. Don't make your Pleaser Time merely work delivered in a different-colored package.

1. *Center Yourself.* Take in three deep breaths of vibrancy. Let out three deep breaths of staleness. Feel yourself centered in your authenticity.

2. *Ask for the Greatest Good.* As Mayor, take a moment and claim your office, and make an enlivening choice for the highest good of all concerned.

3. *Set Your Intention.* Set your intention to discover what delights you.

4. *Open the Window.* Put one hand on your heart. Close your eyes. Invite yourself to let go of your preconceived notions and get curious about what's luscious for you.

5. *Feel the Breeze.* Notice how the wind changes every moment. What's the freshest choice right now? Is it wearing your lime green polka dot socks and orange blouse? Is it finally going to that ping-pong café?

6. *Is It Drive-across-Town Good?* Act like an Italian. Go for the juiciest version. Does it make you giggle with glee? If eating Greek food is your favorite, is it the yummiest in town?

7. *La Dolce Vita.* Life is sweeter if you take time to enjoy it. How about a Pleaser break? Take a bit of time to relish your world every day. Visit a gallery or a pet store, or get the best cup of coffee in town.

8. *Thank Yourself.* Thank yourself for making a fabulous choice to celebrate and enjoy your life.

13

Honey, You Need New Glasses

Gratitude Looks Good on You

You're sitting in a café savoring a creamy chai. After the first few sips, your eyes scan the scene. At the next table is a gal reading a newspaper. She turns the page—and your sale radar goes off. You spy a tiny One Day Only 75% Off Sample Sale ad. It's at that chic boutique that's way out of your budget . . . until now. She notices it too. As you take another sip you can't help but look again. The Sample Sale Ad Gal is moving the paper closer and closer to her face until it almost touches her nose. She is squinting to get the small-print info. Hmm, you think, that girl needs some glasses. Who knows? She might even get a great deal on some trendy new threads if she's wearing a sexy pair of specs.

Actually, there is one eyewear prescription we all need. Though these glasses aren't found in an optometrist's office. Nope. I haven't found a single doc dispensing them. What makes it so crazy is that the world would be a better place if we all wore them. I'm talking about Gratitude Glasses.

Negative focus clouds your sight. Gratitude lets you perceive past what's obvious and find the good. It makes situations pop into a new clarity. Remember my friend Scott, the blind man who helped build a TV network? He taught me the power of gratitude when he said, "If someone offered to give me back my sight, I would turn it down. I've gained so much. I'm such a bigger person for having found the good in being blind. I found a magnificence I couldn't have seen with my eyes."

What gift might become visible to you once you put on the glasses of gratitude?

They Got Out the Magnifying Class

Leave it to some savvy researchers to put gratitude under the microscope. New studies are confirming that all the stuff you thought would make you happy—the turbocharged new car, the two-week jaunt to Bora Bora, the closet full of new shoes—doesn't. An attitude of gratitude turns out to be a bigger predictor of who feels glad to be alive than a big ol' whopping bank account. Yep, just wearing Gratitude Glasses makes the difference.

Happiness cuts across economic lines. Contentment can't tell the difference between a Camry and a Cadillac. Another study found that folks who were appreciative for what they had (whether they had a lot or a little) were as happy as the people who had the most. Wait. It gets even better. The

> Contentment can't tell the difference between a Camry and a Cadillac.

people who were grateful for what they had, even if it wasn't much, were *twice* as happy as those who actually had the most stuff. Ha! What better proof? Get yourself a prescription for a pair of thankfulness lenses and watch your life transform.

In the Research Project on Gratitude and Thanksgiving two researchers put the theory of gratitude to another kind of exam. They asked several hundred people to keep daily journals. The first group jotted down all of the day's occurrences, whether they were good or bad. The second group recorded only the day's lousy experiences. The third group compiled a daily list of only those things for which they were grateful. Hmmmm . . . can you guess the result? You knew it. The grateful group had measurably higher levels of energy, alertness, and determination as well as lower levels of stress and depression. And there's more. They were more likely to feel loved, and they were more likely to engage in acts of kindness toward others. People having more energy, feeling more loved, and being nicer to each other—yes indeed, the Earth would be a better place if everybody wore Gratitude Glasses. And it only takes a second to put them on.

Becky's Story

When Becky first stepped into my office, she was wearing a pair of D&Gs. I'm not talking Dolce and Gabbana. These were bad news sunglasses, and they were dimming her vision so badly she could hardly see. Becky was a restaurant owner, and her first restaurant had established itself very quickly. So when her second restaurant didn't become an overnight sensation too, her confidence got zapped. She was seriously questioning her own qualifications as a restaurateur, and very seriously considering throwing in the towel, selling her first restaurant, and going back to school for a year.

Those Glasses Don't Suit You

If focusing on the lousy fogs up your awareness, then looking for the good clears it up. I'm not talking about the blind stare of a Hollywood bimbo, saying everything is "fine" when it isn't. I think of gratitude as seeing the world through the eyes of your heart. Keep looking for the good and guess what you will discover . . . the good! When you slip on the gratitude spectacles, you shift out of the short-sighted view of how lame things are and begin to see what the heck else might be there.

Crazy as it seems, the situation doesn't have to change. It's simply your perception of it that transforms. Thankfulness sees the greater picture. It gives your attitude some altitude. Don't you figure that, from its vantage point, the Great Good sees that "it's all good" even when you can't? When you take a moment to look at what's bugging you from a higher perspective, the limitations of what you can see fall away.

Back to Becky

Becky realized she needed to take off her D&Gs and put on a good-looking pair of Gratefulness Glasses. I encouraged her to make a gratitude list. She started out with just a few things great and small that she was thankful for—truffles, her mom, French champagne, ping-pong, and sunsets. Through the next month she added more to her list. Things like cinnamon dental floss, having teeth, and Tivo. To anchor the thankfulness practice into her body, her homework was to give herself lots of pats on the back. Real pats on the back. (Hey, you deserve a pat on the back.

Hold your hands in front of you. Now put them on your shoulders. Start patting while you say "I am proud of you." See how good it feels.)

As Becky practiced making gratitude part of her day, her outlook began to shift. She found herself spontaneously thanking the people around her—something she had not done for months. She realized she had lost sight of the kick she got out of serving her delicious concoctions and the camaraderie with her employees— and she wanted it back again.

> *The Fab Five: What are five things you are grateful for right now?*

Heck, she told herself, she was in her early thirties and owned two bistros. How cool was that? It took the sting out of having no take-home pay while she developed her new location.

As her gratitude practice gained momentum, Becky started seeing the challenges of her new location as blessings. Nope, that isn't a typo. She began to see the blessings. The slow growth of the second location was challenging her to manage both restaurants more efficiently. As her attitude changed from panic to thankfulness, Becky felt more ease, and in that ease she became more creative. She realized that (1) a slow beginning doesn't mean failure—she just needed to do a bit more advertising; (2) running a thriving business doesn't require a college degree, but it does require a good bookkeeper; (3) watching where her money went meant that she was managing the flow of energy more wisely.

These solutions were no less available to Becky when she was wearing her smoky shades. Now that she had cleared her vision, she could see them.

Who Gets the Goodie Bag?

Have you heard of the Goodie Bags Theory of the Universe? It's based on the principle that grateful people are magnets for good stuff to come to them. And the best stuff is often not the stuff you can see.

Don't believe me? Let's run a contest called Goodie Bag Giveaway. Fill a goodie bag full of your very favorite things to give away as the prize. Mine would have jasmine and roses from my garden, a slab of Mom's sour cream chocolate cake, a linen robe my sister made, my Happy Girl Go-Go Boots, and three favorite books. What would be in your goodie bag?

Now comes the tough part. Who to give it to? Imagine two contestants standing in front of you. Bachelorette #1 is Bettina. Here's the lowdown on Bettina: Her closet is full of thrift store finds that she lovingly remodels to fit her sturdy frame. Even though she doesn't have a big job or bank balance, most people think of her as one of the richest people they know. When she enters a room you feel better because she radiates happiness. I hear she was just in a fender-bender and told a friend she was grateful that it wasn't worse. Bettina manages to find something good in just about everything. Now Bachelorette #2, Blanche. Blanche is bored, bored, bored. She doesn't need to work because of her rich father. She spends her days power shopping, getting mani-pedis, and doing an occasional yoga class. Even so, she is usually sour about something. She just got back from a two-week vacation on an exotic island off Thailand. Her comment: "It was dull." For Bettina nothing is ever good enough.

So who are you inspired to give all the yummy stuff in your

goodie bag to? There ain't no way my goodies are going to anyone but Bettina. I want my gifts to be appreciated. How about you?

The Universe works on the same principle. The grateful people attract the good luck. (And the people who are always complaining always get more stuff to complain about.) This is not a passive stance. The most successful people are not victims. Even when crappy stuff happens, they find a lesson in it. The real

> *Gratitude gets the Goodie Bag.*
> *Gratitude IS the Goodie Bag.*

fabulistas find a way to take a challenge and use it as a strengthener or a stepping stone to success.

Try out the Goodie Bag Theory. Track the amazing surprises the Universe hands you as you develop your thankfulness response. Let me know what you discover.

Miracles in Gratitude and Appreciation

I consider myself extremely fortunate to have been mentored by one of the world's experts in gratitude and appreciation. Lawrence was so kind and generous that when I first met him I thought he was faking it. He was running an international manufacturing company and an educational foundation. How could he spend an entire lunch helping me with a business problem . . . and then pick up the tab?

I would watch how he handled the intricacies of dealing with his suppliers. Lots of times I wanted to cuss out the very people he was thanking. If a factory missed a deadline, he would say, "Thank you for letting me know. I remember that your father has been ill. How is he?" Like any smart manufacturer, Lawrence had given himself some lead time on the order. Yet his graciousness always paid off. When he really needed a favor, the factory owner was more than eager to help him. He taught me the value of saying thank you in every situation—even the ones that seem to suck.

Once, as the largest order his company had ever handled was about to be shipped, I watched Lawrence blanch as his secretary handed him a fax. The Fortune 500 client had taken a mammoth hit in the stock market. They were cutting their order in half. Since the products he had made already bore their corporate logo, there was absolutely no way to sell them to anyone else.

Rather than screaming and calling in his attorneys (which is what I wanted to do), Lawrence did something I found amazing. He took a moment and put himself in his client's shoes. Lawrence saw the difficult position they were in. Due to the huge loss they could have cancelled the order altogether. He also recognized that a new vice president had recently been assigned to his account, someone who hadn't worked directly with him before. Rather than looking at the difficulties the cancellation posed, he focused on the long-term relationship between the two companies. Lawrence wrote the company a letter thanking them for their loyalty and acknowledging their current tough situation. He looked forward to continuing to do business with them and offered his help in this difficult time.

Appreciation is magic. A few days later, Lawrence got a fax reinstating most of the huge original order.

Slip on Some New Eyewear

Where in your life would a shift of vision do some good?

What would you like to look at through a pair of Gratitude Glasses? Does the mound of work on your desk make you bristle? Slip on those eyeglasses and take a look. Hey, it's great that you have a job (lots of people in the world don't). Find something you like about your office space (they finally got a new coffee maker, the tree outside your window is leafing out, the wise grin of the 10-year-old beaming at you from the picture frame sitting on your desk always makes you smile).

Set your sights to perceive the good hidden in life's challenges and then express your thankfulness for that good. See if something that seemed lousy at first doesn't unfold into something terrific. It's a beautiful life when you look at it through your Gratitude Glasses. Wouldn't the world be a better place if we all wore them?

The Find the Good Game

Finding the good is just a game, like hide and seek. Or an Easter Egg hunt. You can play it all day or for the rest of your life. I sure am. It's a great time to use your GPS and experience your life from a higher vantage point. Your objective is to find as much good as possible even in the funkiest of places.

1. *Center Yourself.* Take in a deep breath of thankfulness. Let out a deep breath of doom and gloom. Do this three times or until you feel more gratitude.

2. *Ask for the Greatest Good.* As Mayor, take a moment

and ask that your vision aligns with the highest good for all.

3. *Set Your Intention.* Set an intention to experience your gratitude.

4. *What a Feeling.* Put your hands on your heart. Connect with the image of what you love deeply. (Your grandma, your puppy, a place in nature. . . .) Feel that warm glow in your heart. Are you thankful that this person or thing is in your life?

5. *Ugh.* Think of a current challenge. Create a specific picture of what is bothering you.

6. *Try on Your Specs.* Now, put on your magic Gratitude Glasses. They give you the power to view your funk through the wise, loving perspective of your heart.

7. *What Do You See?* Look at your funk through the eyes of loving. Find the good. Ask yourself, "How can I use this situation to become better in some way?"

8. *Mirror, Mirror.* Once you are done, go and look in the mirror. Find the good in you.

9. *The Fab 20.* Write a list of 20 things—big or small—you are grateful for.

10. *Hide and Seek.* As you move through your day have fun finding the good. It may show up in places where you least expect it.

11. *Thank Yourself.* Thank yourself for being grateful for the goodie bag that is your life.

14

Vacuums Suck, but Why Should You?

Why Not Make Somebody's Day?

As you peer through your Gratitude Glasses are you starting to see the wonder of this world? In particular, are you noticing how You-ville and All-of-Us-ville are intricately interdependent? Feeling part of and contributing to the great Us-ville of this beautiful planet is so natural to your nature that it's good for you. Besides, success is merely a dusty trophy sitting on a shelf if you don't share it. Simply snatching what you want without thinking of others leaves you always wanting more. Just like a vacuum.

Think about it. A vacuum cleaner sucks. That's its job. But what a life. Its mission is snorting dirt. The only direction it looks is down. And its insatiable thirst for filth is never satisfied. Tiny particles of dust settle back onto the carpet even before the vacuuming is done.

> *Success is just a dusty trophy sitting on a shelf if you don't share it.*

A vacuum doesn't give; it only takes. No wonder it sits alone in the closet most of the time. I figure it's got to be a pretty grumpy household appliance. It exists only to inhale cat hair and cake crumbs. How rosy a world is that?

Even though you have a lot of savvy success strategies under your belt, let's face it: you're a human being. There are times when you get stuck in a funk about the gunk of your day. Instead of savoring your life and accomplishing your goals, you start sorting through your problems. And more than likely it looks like they're somebody else's fault. Someone did you wrong. Bad-wrong. They tracked in the mud of their dreadful behavior all over the nice, clean cashmere-toned Berber carpet of your life. You glom onto the problem. You go over it again and again and again and again. You're so fixated on plucking up the crud left behind that you forget what you wanted in the first place.

You're caught in Vacuum Victim Mode. And when you're in VVM you are in Funkytown—and not the kicky disco version. You have temporary amnesia that you are the Mayor and have the clout to create your day. You don't think you can flip the switch. That's where the miracle comes in.

The best way to climb out of the vacuum bag of "woe is me" is to do something for somebody else. I know, I know . . . that Feel Sorry Soiree feels as comfortable as sweat pants and old slippers. Crawling out of it seems as counterintuitive as putting on your party pants when all you want to do is curl up under the covers. But believe me, it works. Give someone else a helping hand. You'll forget that you were ever in a Blah Fest to begin with.

I Heart Sharing

Science is backing me up on this one. Researchers have been

identifying tons of benefits that come from contributing to others. For one thing, helping others is good for your physical health. Studies report that people involved in ongoing volunteer programs show an enhanced immune system, improved cardiovascular circulation, and better sleep patterns. That isn't too shabby.

But wait, there's more. Giving has emotional benefits, too. Folks who are busy serving others have a sense of control over their circumstances, increased ability to cope with crises, and stronger feelings of personal satisfaction, compassion, and empathy. That doesn't suck either.

And there are still more benefits. Helping others may be a key factor in living longer. In one study, Dr. Stephanie Brown and her colleagues at the Institute for Social Research at the University of Michigan tracked 423 older couples over a five-year period. The people who reported that they were *not* lending a hand to others were *more than twice* as likely to die during those five years as those who did. Wow. A simple act like driving your neighbor to the auto shop to pick up her car gives you a 50 percent chance of living longer.

The Bad Hair Day Buster

Okay. Okay. Okay. You know it's the right thing to do. But you are too dang busy. You're swamped. You have been trying to get your own car to the repair shop for three weeks. You don't have the time to help out somebody else. Plus, you are having a Bad Hair Day. Phew, I can relate.

The remedy for feeling lousy is to give a gift to someone else. It doesn't matter what it is, as long as you aren't demanding something in return. Putting conditions on a gift makes it a negotiation instead of an act of service. You'll find giving for the simple joy of it far more fulfilling. Nothing can turn a Bad Hair Day around like helping someone in need. And like anything else, you can break it down to make it happen. You don't need to sign up for the Peace Corps to be of service. Smiling and saying a genuine thank you to the checkout clerk takes no time. Zipping off a thank you card or calling a sick friend falls in the under-two-minute category. Giving someone a footrub takes under ten minutes.

> *Nothing turns a Bad Hair Day around like helping someone.*

Get High on Helping

That feel-good feeling that comes from giving to someone else is so well-recognized that researchers have given it its own moniker: "the helper's high." Don't you just love the name?

You know that exercise is a terrific way to de-stress yourself. You know how good you feel right after a long run or a kick-butt workout. That's because strenuous exercise releases endorphins. Those endorphins create an elated feeling known as the runner's high—even though a person has been exerting themselves, they don't feel stressed and tired, they feel more relaxed and joyous. A British research team found that even moderate exercise raised the levels of phenylethylmine, or PEA, a chemical in the brain that improves mood. Even on the following day, over 80 percent of the participants still had higher levels of PEA. Altruistic giving apparently gives your body that same boost. In a different study, a charity in New York City conducted a survey of 3,300 volunteers. Many reported having feelings of euphoria while they were taking part in the charity's service project. In fact, they reported having more energy at the end of a long day of serving others than they started with at the beginning of the day.

A Money-Back Guarantee

Why not give it a go? Put a $1 Fab Pack in your car or purse. Take $1 worth of coins and put them in parking meters that are about to expire. If you do that for three days and don't feel genuinely better about yourself, write me a letter and I'll refund your $3 investment. I am willing to put money on the table that giving makes you feel great. And giving anonymously makes you feel even greater.

Take a Fab Five Minutes and make someone's day. There are so many people in need in your community and in our world. You could make a real difference in someone's life. Donating to a charity online could take you under five minutes. Even five dollars could help someone somewhere.

Being of service has a double benefit. Helping someone in need can't help but make you feel good. It helps someone else, and it shifts you too.

It's Never Too Late

While completing this book, I spent a few days with my wonderful editor in a place that seemed close to paradise. Our writing retreat was in the hills above Santa Barbara—a place of special quiet with a mystical evening hour. As the sun starts to set the oak groves are saturated with a golden light that paints every bush the color of heaven. I felt embraced like a friend in this place. I wondered if it called me there so I could tell its story.

The retreat house had been built by a 90-year-old woman as a gift. She had lived her long life on the East Coast. Her husband had passed away, and she longed to spend her golden years in the golden light of Santa Barbara overlooking the sea. Friend after friend rolled their eyes as she told them of her plans. She was 90 years old, for goodness sake! But the minor detail of being ten years shy of a century wasn't going to stop her.

> *Get out of the way and let kindness have its say.*

Even if her friends were moving into assisted living facilities, she was going to create something fabulous.

She moved to Santa Barbara and rented a small place nearby while her dream house was being built so she could oversee the project herself. The petite white-haired lady surrounded by burly construction workers must have been quite a sight. It probably wasn't the easiest time of her life, but creating her vision seemed to give her the vigor of a far younger gal.

Talk about how giving boosts your health—once the house was completed, this generous and vibrant woman lived in it for almost a decade. Deeply interested in others, she cultivated friendships with people of all ages. And they loved her. She died peacefully in her sleep a few days before her hundredth birthday. She left the house to the retreat center to share with others—no strings attached.

Her house did teach me. It's never too late to create the life you want. You are never too old or too frail to give, whether it's a house or something as simple as a smile. This woman's kindness welcomed this stranger, someone she had never met, with open arms. What a world it would be if we greeted each other with such goodwill. What a blessed place our planet would be if you and I did a little something every day to make it better than we found it.

Fully You

By now you've learned that as Mayor of You-ville you have the power to sway your day. You've gotten to know the brilliance of You-ville and maybe found out that God is the kinda guy you can trust. You've defrosted your TV dinner reality and hopefully are burning your brownies less often.

There's no shortage of fabulous once you begin to see it and cultivate it. What are you going to do with it all? Why not share it? Why not serve the greater good? Besides, it's a great way to go from grump to goddess when the need arises. Hey, there is probably someone in the world who could use a bit of your kindness right now.

This moment is waiting for you to color it the way you choose. Right now you can get unstuck. You can get out of your own way and let your dreams have their say. You can create the life you want. Even if you're 90.

Putting aside funk and choosing fabulous is easy. Because fabulous is who you already and always are.

The Gift of Giving Game

Now that you have spent time filling up with the glorious goodness of who you really are, the next natural step is to share it. Playing this game can help make the world one big Club Fabulous.

1. *Center Yourself.* Take in three deep breaths of sharing your goodness Let out three deep breaths of selfishness. Brava!

2. *Ask for the Greater Good.* As Mayor, take a moment and claim your office, and ask to serve others for the highest good of all concerned.

3. *Set Your Intention.* Set your intention to offer a helping hand to someone.

4. *Fab 15.* Take 15 minutes to make somebody's day. Focus on serving others. See how many people you can touch. Or how significantly you can impact one life. Buy a stranger a cup of coffee, donate to a charity, put a quarter in someone else's parking meter.

5. *Doing Does It.* Serving another is loving in action. It doesn't matter what you do as long as you aren't looking for something in return.

6. *Thank Yourself.* Thank yourself. The world thanks you for making a fabulous choice and making this Earth a better place. One choice at a time.

Acknowledgments

Thank you to:

My wonderful, wonderous, big-hearted family. I love you, plain and simple.

Drs. Ron and Mary Hulnick and the folks at the University of Santa Monica, for encouraging me to share my vibrant colors.

Dr. Jean Houston, for slapping me on the knee and being the midwife for my journey as an author.

Barbara Holden, for being the best friend I could ever hope for. Ever. Ever. Ever.

David and Kathryn Allen, Bertrand and Roberta Babinet, John and Marion Bateman, Andra Curasso, Nicholas Brown, and Martha Ringer, for seeing me through the Bad Hair Years into the Big Hair Years.

Prudence Fenton, for your extraordinary vision, support, and partnership. I won't forget that it's three. I hope to be part of four, five, and six.

John Mason Esq., how fortunate I am to have your incredible guidance and support.

Mark Zuckerman, for being my cultural attaché and dear friend.

Carolyn Bond, for being an editor committed to the excellence of this project. This is a better book because of you.

Beth Hansen-Winter for your wonderful design. What a treat to work with you.

Brenda Fishbaugh, for being the TLC inspiration that you are!

The best doctors in California for your ongoing support: Jeffrey Hirsch, M.D., Phillip Conwisar, M.D., Bruce Broukhim, M.D., James Styner, M.D., and Barry Halote, Ph.D. You are the best!

Stephanie Gunning, for all your early work, guidance, and feisty vision.

Blake Snyder, for being a phenomenal cheerleader.

Mimi Donaldson, for being such a glorious pal and lousy driver.

Cirelle Raphalian, for seeing this books years before I had any clue.

Dr. Andrew Jacobs, for introducing me to the concepts of sports psychology and Turkey Legs.

John Tarnoff, for being my long lost Big Brother back in The Day.

Rick Kanter and Richard Katz, for reminding me of my humble beginnings and never letting me live down having designed the Remote Control Holder.

John Roger, for your ever-present inspiration, loving, and guidance.

John Morton, for showing me that God is the kinda guy I can trust.

All the great folks at Anatomy Entertainment for all your help.

Elena, Isabella, Gian Paolo, and Chiara, for playing shoe store, learning to withstand peanut butter, re-teaching me to ice skate, and not making too much fun of my Italian. Yes, that is a hint.

Annette and Sheldon Bull, thank you for adopting me and showing me what a great marriage looks like.

Acknowledgments

Gracie, for your astonishing generosity of heart.

Jackie Castor, if I ever get to wear a ring on the fourth finger of my left hand, it will probably be because of what you have done.

Park Kerr, for being my man in Texas.

Frank Maguire, for reminding me that the main thing is the main thing.

Dawna Shuman, for your intrepid public relations.

My pals at the Gold Coast Institute, for their ongoing support.

Joan Stewart, for your terrific PR mentorship. You are the best, best, best!

Irina Dragut, for being the best darn intern ever.

Ellen Kleiner and Yolanda Muhammad, blessings to you for all your help in birthing this baby.

A humble thanks to each one of my astonishing and inspiring coaching clients.

And a big honking thanks to YOU for buying this book. If you are reading the acknowledgments, you earn a special place in Club Fabulous!

References

Books

Allen, David. *Getting Things Done: The Art of Stress-Free Productivity.* New York: Penguin Books, 2003.

Baker, Dan, and Cameron Stauth. *What Happy People Know: How the New Science of Happiness Can Change Your Life for the Better.* Emmaus, PA: Rodale Inc., 2003.

Barinov, Zelma. *How to Make Instant Decisions and Remain Happy & Sane—Using Your Inner Compass.* Bala Cynwyd, PA: Access Press, 1998.

Baskin, Elizabeth Cogswell. *How to Run Your Business Like a Girl: Successful Strategies from Entrepreneurial Women Who Made It Happen.* Avon, MA: Adams Media, 2005.

Brumberg, Joan Jacobs. *The Body Project: An Intimate History of American Girls.* New York: Random House, 1997.

Chandler, Steve, and Scott Richardson. *100 Ways to Motivate Others: How Great Leaders Can Produce Insane Results without Driving People Crazy.* Franklin Lakes, NJ: Career Press, 2005.

De Beauport, Elaine, with Aura Sofia Diaz. *The Three Faces of Mind: Developing Your Mental, Emotional, and Behavioral Intelligences.* Wheaton, IL: Quest Books, 1996.

Girsch, Maria, and Charlie Girsch. *Fanning the Creative Spirit.* St. Paul: Creativity Central, 2001.

Hanley, Jesse Lynn, and Nancy Deville. *Tired of Being Tired: Rescue, Repair, Rejuvenate.* New York: Penguin Putnam Inc., 2001.

Hendricks, Gay, and Kathlyn Hendricks. *Conscious Loving: The Journey to Co-Commitment.* New York: Bantam Books, 1992.

Houston, Jean. *The Search for the Beloved.* New York: Penguin Putnam, 1997.

Lark, Susan M., and James A. Richards. *The Chemistry of Success: Six Secrets of Peak Performance.* San Francisco: Bay Books, 2000.

Leyden-Rubenstein, Lori A. *The Stress Management Handbook: Strategies for Health and Inner Peace.* New Canaan, CT: Keats Publishing, 1998.

Morton, John. *The Blessings Already Are.* Los Angeles: Mandeville Press, 2000.

Muller, Wayne. *Legacy of the Heart: The Spiritual Advantages of a Painful Childhood.* New York: Simon & Schuster, 1993.

Myss, Caroline. *Anatomy of the Spirit: The Seven Stages of Power and Healing.* New York: Three Rivers Press, 1996.

Niven, David. *The 100 Simple Secrets of Happy People: What Scientists Have Learned and How You Can Use It.* San Francisco: HarperCollins, 2000.

Peirce, Penney. *The Intuitive Way: A Guide to Living from Inner Wisdom.* Hillsboro, OR: Beyond Words Publishing, 1997.

Richardson, Cheryl. *Life Makeovers: 52 Practical and Inspiring Ways to Improve Your Life One Week at a Time.* New York: Broadway Books, 2002.

Roger, John. *God Is Your Partner.* Los Angeles: Mandeville Press, 1990.

Roger, John, with Paul Kaye. *Momentum—Letting Love Lead: Simple Practices for Spiritual Living.* Los Angeles: Mandeville Press, 2003.

Waterhouse, Debra. *Outsmarting the Female Fat Cell: The First Weight-Control Program Designed Specifically for Women.* New York: Warner Books, Inc., 1994.

Weinstein, Matt. *Managing to Have Fun: How Fun at Work Can Motivate Your Employees, Inspire Your Coworkers, Boost Your Bottom Line.* New York: Simon & Schuster Inc., 1997.

Articles

ABC TV Diet expert. ABC 7 Chicago. "Want To Lose Weight? Cheat On Your Diet." December 29, 2005. http://abclocal.go.com/wls/story?section=health&id=3768161.

"Americans Have Fewer Friends Outside the Family, Duke Study Shows." *Duke University News & Communications*, August 20, 2006. http://www.dukenews.duke.edu/2006/06/socialisolation.html.

Belluck, Pam. "Nuns Offer Clues to Alzheimer's and Aging." *New York Times*, May 7, 2001. www.stpt.usf.edu/~jsokolov/agealzh2.htm.

Benson, Herbert, Julie Corliss, and Geoffrey Cowley. "Brain Check." *Newsweek* 144:13 (2004): 45–47.

Caine, Renate Nummela, and Geoffrey Caine. *Making Connections: Teaching and the Human Brain*. Nashville, TN: Incentive Publications, 1990. Excerpt available at: www.buffalostate.edu/orgs/bcp/brainbasics/triune.html.

Case Western Reserve University. "Talking in 'Genderlects'." *HR Quarterly*, March 30, 2000. http://www.cwru.edu/finadmin/humres/admin/genderlect.html.

Collins, Anne. "Best Vitamins for Weight Reduction." http://www.annecollins.com/best-vitamins-for-weight-control.htm. 2000–2005.

Counseling Center, University of Illinois. "Self-help Brochures." http://www.couns.uiuc.edu/Brochures/perfecti.htm. 10/25/2005.

DeNoon, Daniel. "Is 'Runner's High' a Cure For Depression?" *WebMD*, August 20, 2006. Original article September 27, 2001. http://www.webmd.com/content/article/34/1728_90004.

Emmons, Robert A., and Michael E. McCullough. "Highlights from the Research Project on Gratitude and Thankfulness: Dimensions and Perspectives of Gratitude." http://psychology.ucdavis.edu/labs/emmons/.

Estabrook, Alison. "12 Leaders on Life Lessons." *Newsweek* 146:17 (2005): 70–76.

Gaouette, Nicole. "Gut Instinct Gets Scientific on Border." *Los Angeles Times*, June 26, 2005.

Gates, Chee. "The Talking Cure." *O Magazine* (December 2004): 206.

Gibbs, Nancy. "Midlife Crisis? Bring It On!" *Time* 165:20 (2005): 52–63.

Greenberg, Neil. "The Beast at Play: The Neuroethology of Creativity." https://notes.utk.edu/bio/greenberg.nsf/9e9a470d5230cdda85 2563ef0059fa56/ff73036755b1490685256b4b000570fc?Open

Document. Originally published in *The Child's Right to Play: A Global Approach,* 309–327, eds. Rhonda Clements and Leah Fiorentino (Westport, CT: Praeger Press, 2004).

Hanlon, Kathie. "What Is the Relationship between Low Self-Esteem and Eating Disorders?" http://www.vanderbilt.edu/AnS/psychology/health_psychology/esteem.htm. 08/30/04.

Hassen, Farrah. "Sleep Deprivation: Effects on Safety, Health and the Quality of Life." http://communications.fullerton.edu/facilities/tvfilm_studios/content/safety/sleep.htm. 2002.

Healy, Melissa. "Our Innate Need for Friendship." *Los Angeles Times,* May 9, 2005.

Hotz, Robert Lee. "Deep, Dark Secrets of His and Her Brains." *Los Angeles Times,* June 16, 2005.

"The Importance of B-Group Vitamins." 101 Lifestyle.com. http://www.101lifestyle.com/health/vitaminb2.html. 2004.

Kalb, Claudia. 2004. "Buddha Lessons." *Newsweek* 144:13 (2004): 48–51.

Kantrowitz, Barbara. "When Women Lead." *Newsweek* 146:17 (2005): 46–47.

Kazlev, M. Alan. "The Triune Brain." www.kheper.net/topics/intelligence/MacLean.htm., October 19, 2003.

"Know Your Vitamins." Medical Explorer. http://www.medical-explorer.com/vitamins.php.

MacGregor, Hilary E. "In Need of a Friend." *Los Angeles Times,* June 26, 2006.

MacLean, Paul D. "Expanding Lifespan Learning." www.newhorizons.org/future/Creating_the_Future/crfut_maclean.html.

Michael, Yvonne L., Graham A. Colditz, Eugenie Coakley, and Ichiro Kawachi. "Health Behaviors, Social Networks, and Healthy Aging: Cross-Sectional Evidence from the Nurses' Health Study." *Quality of Life Research Harvard Medical School* 8:8 (1999): 711–722.

Mundell, E. J. "Sitcoms, Videos Make Even Fifth-Graders Feel Fat." Natural Solutions Radio. www.naturalsolutionsradio.com/articles/article.html?id=2817&filter. 03/24/06.

News with CNN. "Why Women Can't Read Maps." http://cnn. netscape.cnn.com/news/package.jsp?name=fte/womenmaps/ womenmaps. 2006.

Parker-Pope, Tara: "The Secrets of Successful Ageing." Neurological Foundation of New Zealand, Neurological News. http://www. neurological.org.nz/html/article.php?documentCode=1338.June 20, 2005.

Pinker, Steven. "How to Think about the Mind." *Newsweek* 144:13 (2004): 78.

Puppetools: Advancing the Language of Play. "Play Tectonics." www. puppetools.com/?p=playtectonics. See also: www.puppetools. com/ kids_workshop/?p=paul.

"Riboflavin." Wikipedia: The Free Encyclopedia. http://en.wikipedia. org/wiki/Vitamin_G 16:52. June, 27 2006.

Segelken, Roger. "Maas: National (Sleep) Debt Is Killing Americans, Hurting Economy." *Cornell Chronicle.* http://www.news.cornell.edu/ Chronicle/98/1.22.98/sleep_debt.html. January 22, 1998.

Signorielli, N. (1997, April). "Reflections of Girls in the Media: A Two-Part Study on Gender and Media. National Institute on Media and the Family. http://www.mediafamily.org/facts/facts_mediaeffect. shtml. 09/01/04.

Taylor, Shelley E., Laura Cousino Klein, Brian P. Lewis, Tara L. Gruenewald, Regan A. R. Gurung, and John A. Updegraff. "Biobehavioral Responses to Stress in Females: Tend-and Befriend, Not Fight-or-Flight." *Psychological Review* 107:3 (2000): 411–429. http://bbh.hhdev.psu.edu/labs/bbhsl/PDF%20files/taylor%20et%20al.% 202000.pdf.

Tiggemann, M., and A. S. Pickering. "Role of Television in Adolescent Women's Body Dissatisfaction and Drive for Thinness." *International Journal of Eating Disorders,* 20 (1996): 199–203.

"UCLA Researchers Identify Key Biobehavioral Pattern Used by Women to Manage Stress." *Science Daily,* May 22, 2000. http://www. sciencedaily.com/releases/2000/05/000522082151.htm.

Underwood, Anne. "For a Happy Heart." *Newsweek* 144:13 (2004): 54–56.

Warner, Judith. "Mommy Madness." *Newsweek,* February 21, 2006. http://www.msnbc.msn.com/id/6959880/site/newsweek/.

Winfrey, Oprah. "A Little Restoration Goes a Long Way." *O Magazine* (July 2004): 190.

———. "How I Got There." *Newsweek* 146:17 (2005): 48–49.

Women's Sports Foundation. "Too Many Girls Are Not Physically or Psychologically Healthy, Happy or Confident about Their Ability to Succeed in Life." https://www.womenssportsfoundation.org/binary-data/WSF_ARTICLE/pdf_file/984.pdf.

Welcome to Club Fabulous

Congratulations! Now that you've read *Funky to Fabulous,* you are a member of Club Fabulous! Welcome to a community of "Fabulous People Coming Together to Live Their Fabu-Lives."

It will be great to stay in touch with you! Stop by www.FunkytoFabulous.com to say hello, stay connected, and stay tuned for a Club Fabulous meeting near you! Keep us posted with the funky, the fabulous, and whatever else is going on in You-ville.

Speaking of You-ville. . . . You-ville, Me-ville, and Us-ville are connected, so please share this book with five of your most fabulous friends. Let's make the world one big Club Fabulous.

PLEASE SEND ME MORE *FUNKY TO FABULOUS* BOOKS.
$24.95 hardcover. I understand that I may return any of them
for a full refund for any reason, no questions asked.

EMAIL ORDERS: orders@funkytofabulous.com

POSTAL ORDERS: Oak Grove Publishing
269 South Beverly Drive, Suite 248
Beverly Hills, CA 90212

Please send me FREE information on the following:

☐ Other products   ☐ Speaking   ☐ Coaching
☐ Tele-Seminars   ☐ Club Fabulous

Name _____

Address _____

City _____ State _____ Zip _____

Telephone _____

Email address _____

SALES TAX: Please add 7.75% for all products
shipped to a California address.

SHIPPING:

U.S.: Please add $4.50 for first book or CD,
and $2.50 for each additional product.

International: $10.00 for first book or CD, and
$5.00 for each additional product (estimate).

Funky to Fabulous